A WEALTH OF MUSIC

A WEALTH OF MUSIC

in the collections of the
British Library (Reference Division)
and the British Museum

Alec Hyatt King

CLIVE BINGLEY  LONDON

Published by Clive Bingley Limited, 16 Pembridge Road, London W11, and printed and bound in England by Redwood Burn Limited, Trowbridge, Wiltshire.

First published 1983

British Library Cataloguing in Publication Data

King, Alec Hyatt
A wealth of music.
1. British Library — Reference Division
2. Music
I. Title
016.91 Z921.B854
ISBN 0-85157-330-4

Typeset by Allset in 11 on 12 point Journal Roman

1234568786858483

CONTENTS

habet tempus pagina quaeque suum

Ausonius

FOREWORD

The idea of this book came to me many years ago, quite early in my service as Superintendent of the Music Room in the British Museum. At that time the Director's Office was in the habit of sending to the Music Room, which formed part of the Department of Printed Books, numerous postal enquiries about anything to do with music. Those which were too specialised for me and my staff to answer we passed on to the appropriate department of the Museum. It also fell to me to organize, with the help of various colleagues, a considerable number of exhibitions (some with published catalogues, which are listed on p.44). Many of them included items of musical interest drawn from departments other than those of Printed Books and Manuscripts. Such items could sometimes be traced from published departmental catalogues, but often they had not been recorded in this way, and their presence in the collections was known only to a few specialists.

Gradually, I began to divine the extent of the musical material in the museum's collections. For besides what was to be found in the Departments of Printed Books and of Manuscripts, other departments contained much else – iconography, representations of many kinds of performance in many countries and periods, documents and records relating to musical history, and a number of musical instruments. Moreover, much of this wealth of music, in the widest sense of the term, seemed to be unique, and some of it little known. But I also realized that it would be impracticable to compile a complete record of it. I felt, however, that a selective account, partly in continuous prose and partly in lists of various kinds, would at least provide a work of ready reference, and a basis for further enquiry.

This idea long lay dormant, and it was only after my retirement in 1976 that I could begin to give it my systematic attention. But before then there had occurred the first of the events which were to affect the earlier plan of the book. This was the British Library Act of July 1972, which came into force a year later. The effect of this Act was twofold. It removed from the jurisdiction of the Trustees of the

British Museum the three library departments, ie Printed Books, Manuscripts, and Oriental Manuscripts and Printed Books, although their collections and staff were for the most part to remain in the Museum's precincts until a new building could be provided. The Act also combined the three departments with some other organizations – notably the National Central Library, the National Lending Library for Science and Technology and the British National Bibliography – to form the British Library, administered by the British Library Board.

The second event was the proposal, submitted to the Board in 1979 by K. G. Saur and ratified by contract in 1980, to publish for the first time in a unified form the diverse catalogues of printed music. (The history of these catalogues up to c.1920 is related in my book *Printed Music in the British Museum*, published by Clive Bingley Ltd in 1979.) Previously, what was by far the largest of these catalogues, that of the music printed since 1800, had been available only for consultation in Bloomsbury. But unified publication for world-wide use called for a rather different approach in the present volume from what I had originally planned.

While these events caused me to modify the plan and presentation of my work in some essentials, they did not alter its extent and purpose. Most of the special collections I intended to describe had been built up as part of the same unique whole during a period of well over two centuries.

It also seemed likely that, with one or two exceptions, they would remain under one roof for some time after my book appeared, pending the construction of the new building for the British Library on the Euston Road site. Moreover, after its ultimate completion and the removal of the books, the British Museum would still not be very far away. Even if the two institutions had not been administratively separated, the proportions of what must now be two distinct sections of this book would have been the same.

In presenting the information about the museum departments, I have been guided by several principles. Where there is a published catalogue or guide devoted wholly to musical objects, their range can generally be judged from the title of the book and the note I have added to summarize its contents. There are other catalogues, published and unpublished, of special collections containing a fair number of musical objects which may not be specified in the title. These I have treated in two ways. I have either summarized the contents in a note or have listed the relevant items more or less according to the descriptions given in the catalogue. Some departments contain musical objects that are not recorded in any catalogue. Here I have listed them individually, grouped as required according to types, and have always added the registration number – or in some cases the shelf number – of each, to facilitate identification. Other objects, again, though included in a catalogue, may be so very few in relation to an extremely large special collection, that it seemed reasonable to list these also individually and not under the title of any publication.

The nature of the musical objects is as diverse as the collections in which they are to be found, and this diversity is reflected in the variety of ways in which they have been described. Consequently, it seemed impracticable to treat all of them with rigid consistency. But I hope that the fairly generous indexes will compensate for any anomalies and inconsistencies, and will, in addition, unify the material scattered throughout the British Museum and link it to whatever may be congruent in the collections of the British Library.

The Reference Division of the Library poses some problems of a different kind, the chief one being due to the heterogeneous nature and irregular disposition of some of the musical material in the Department of Printed Books. For instance, by far the largest part of the musical literature is to be found in the General Library of this department. But there is a substantial and important quantity of such books in the Hirsch Music Library and a smaller amount in the Royal Music Library, both of which consist largely of music. But both these collections had been catalogued as entities and for historical reasons their integrity is paramount. Consequently their respective holdings of musical literature could not be physically removed and placed with such books in the General Library. While they remain within the

Music Library, which is responsible for their care and administration, they have all been entered in the *General Catalogue of Printed Books.* Similar considerations apply, *mutatis mutandis*, to the manuscripts, those in the Royal Music being numerous and of the highest importance, while those in the Hirsch Library are relatively few. (The same principle also applies to the manuscripts in the library of the Madrigal Society, likewise housed in the Music Library.)

Given the integrity of the Hirsch and Royal collections, and the fact that their original catalogues had been produced as entities, it seemed reasonable that the listing of them (and, in the case of the Hirsch Library, of the two Accessions Parts produced by the British Museum) should be done under the heading of that section of the library responsible for them, namely the Music Library. It also seemed logical (though perhaps anomalous) that my account of the manuscripts in 'Royal' and 'Hirsch' should be appended to that portion of the book describing the 'scope' of the collections of printed music, rather than to the corresponding one for the Department of Manuscripts. I have applied the same principle to the printed and engraved material preserved in the Department of Manuscripts, and have listed it among their collections. Again the link with identical material elsewhere will be found in the index.

Here perhaps I may explain the nature and purpose of the sections entitled 'The scope of the collections . . . ' In them I have given a necessarily selective account of some of the most interesting and important items, or groups of items, in the several collections. I hope that this may offer some indication of their character to the users of this book, especially to those who may not have immediate access to the principal catalogues. Perhaps this will also assist those who have the catalogues, but may be unfamiliar with the contents and their treatment.

One minor difficulty was to decide in which section of the book the various musical exhibition catalogues could best be brought together. All the exhibitions were mounted before 1973 (ie before the British Library Act came into force) and, as mentioned earlier, a number of them drew on the resources not only of the Departments of Printed Books and of Manuscripts, but on those of other departments of the Museum as well. Most of the exhibitions were initiated by the Music Room, which was part of the Department of Printed Books, and all the major ones were shown in the King's Library, its principal exhibition gallery. So it seemed reasonable to list them together as a special group under that department. There are numerous other catalogues, published and unpublished, listed throughout this book. They vary much in range and purpose. Considered as a whole they provide a valuable first line of enquiry for musical material.

The growth of the collections of the three original Departments of the Reference Division has been marked, as already mentioned, by anomalies which derive largely from their antecedents as part of the British Museum. Some of the framework and details of this book in turn reflect these anomalies. But I trust that here too the index will help to minimize them, and that the book will be useful to all who use the collections, directly or otherwise, for research into any aspect of the art and science of music.

Throughout, it should be noted that all books cited without imprint were published by the Trustees of the British Museum.

ACKNOWLEDGEMENTS

The information given in this book has been amassed in various ways. Within the Reference Division of the British Library I have relied on my own knowledge of the Department of Printed Books (including both the General Library and the Music Library) and of the Department of Manuscripts. Mr Arthur Searle, Assistant Keeper in the latter department, kindly read the relevant section of the book in typescript and made some valuable suggestions. In the Department of Oriental Manuscripts and Printed Books, the published catalogues are numerous, but principally cover printed books, and the Keeper, Dr Geoffrey Marrison, gave me the generous guidance of his staff largely in respect of manuscripts. For the specifications of musical patents in the Holborn Branch of the Science Reference Library, I am indebted to the staff of its reading room, who pointed the way beyond the small number of such publications available in Bloomsbury.

Within the British Museum my indebtedness is generally of a similar kind. The many catalogues, published and unpublished, of the Department of Prints and Drawings provided most of my material in this field. I am grateful to Mr Antony Griffiths, Deputy Keeper, and Mr Reginald Williams, Senior Research Assistant, for some further assistance. In all the other departments of the museum, the number of catalogues which record items of musical interest is relatively small, and in only two departments – those of Greek and Roman Antiquities and of Mediaeval and Later Antiquities – had I some previous personal knowledge of their contents. For these museum departments, as for all the others, I am most grateful to their Keepers for allowing me to consult their staff, whose expertise has been invaluable. I am happy to express my thanks to: Mr R. A. Carson (Coins and Medals); Mr Brian Cook (Greek and Roman Antiquities); Mr Neil Stratford (Mediaeval and Later Antiquities); Dr Ian Longworth (Prehistoric and Romano-British Antiquities); Mr

T. G. H. James (Egyptian Antiquities); Mr M. D. McLeod (Ethnography); Mr Lawrence Smith (Oriental Antiquities); Dr Edmond Sollberger (Western Asiatic Antiquities).

The responsibility for any inadequacies or errors rests solely with myself.

A. H. K.
London, July 1982

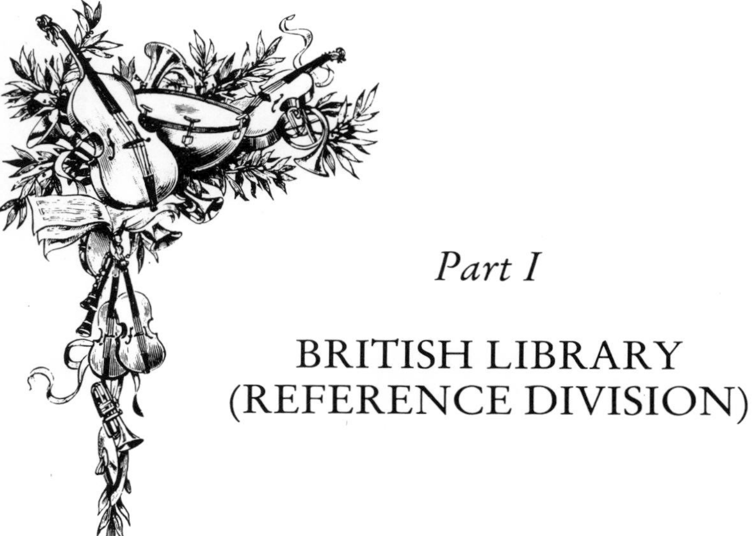

Part I

BRITISH LIBRARY (REFERENCE DIVISION)

DEPARTMENT OF PRINTED BOOKS
Music Library

THE CATALOGUES

Catalogue of Printed Music, etc.

Catalogue of Printed Music in the British Library to 1980. 1 [etc.] A-ANDER [etc.] K. G. Saur: London, München, New York, Paris, 1981 – . To be completed in sixty-two volumes: here referred to as *CPM.*

As mentioned in the preface to vol. 1 p.[vii], signed by O. W. Neighbour, *CPM* originated in the catalogue of printed music in the British Museum (after 1973, the British Library), which took shape from the late eighteenth century onwards. The complex history of these catalogues and their constituent parts is fully described in the present writer's book *Printed Music in the British Museum. An account of the catalogues, the collections and their formation up to 1920* (Clive Bingley, 1979). Here it will suffice to say that among the earlier catalogues subsumed into *CPM* were half a dozen which were printed and published at intervals from 1912 to 1962. Some comprised the contents of particular libraries which the British Museum acquired by gift or purchase, or which were deposited on loan. Others record music of a special period or type. A full description of all of them in their historical context will be found on pages 5 to 9 of the present book.

CPM is based upon two sets of principles the first of which governs the various types of headings ('entry points'), and the second the arrangement of the entries within these headings. These principles and their practical application are fully expounded, with selected examples, in the four pages of the preliminaries [pp.ix-xii] to volume 1 of *CPM* (reprinted in all subsequent volumes) headed 'Guide to the arrangement of entries' (printed anonymously but written by Malcolm Turner).

The information is given as follows:

1 Entry points
2 Choice of main heading
Composers
Pseudonymous works
Anonymous works
Single songs
Preferential headings
Periodicals
3 Cross references
4 Arrangement of headings
5 Arrangement of entries within each heading.
6 Content of individual entries.

What follows here offers some supplementary information on various points in sections 1, 2 and 5.

1 The phrase 'person or body with the primary intellectual responsibility for the work' may be extended to cover groups of popular performers who, collectively or individually, wrote the words and music of songs. Thus the albums of songs performed by the 'Beatles' are entered under that group, with a general cross-reference to it from the name of each of its members.

2 'Preferential headings' – others are CHRISTY MINSTRELS, EASTER CAROLS. In the preferential headings PSALMS and HYMNS, there is one important exception to the general arrangement according to the language of the text. Such publications issued in the United States of America are entered under PSALMS [American] and HYMNS [American].

5 'Arrangements, etc'. In certain headings, eg BEETHOVEN, there is one group of publications, sketchbooks, and the like, which stands between 'Thematic catalogues' and 'Collected editions'.

The 'Appendix of cross-references' – the last group of entries under the name of a composer – may include several different kinds of reference within a single alphabetical sequence, following the word 'See'. These may comprise references:

(a) to the name of another composer in respect of editorial work;

(b) to the name of the editor of an anthology;

(c) to the name of another composer in respect of a work embodying or based on part or whole of two or more identified works of the original composer;
(d) to the name of another composer in respect of a work embodying or based on a single unidentified work of the original composer.

Two points deserve mention within the general alphabetical sequence:

(i) A facsimile, complete or partial, of any single work precedes all editions of it;
(ii) Under 'concertos', works for two or more solo instruments precede those for a single solo instrument, and those for the latter are arranged alphabetically under the conventional English name of the instrument, irrespective of period.

Liturgies, ie unharmonized music, of whatever rite or church, are not entered in *CPM*. They are, however, to be found in the *General Catalogue of Printed Books* (all editions) under the heading LITURGIES, which is arranged according to rites and churches. Here, entries for books which contain music are distinguished, in those cases where the title does not make the fact clear, by the addition in square brackets, of the phrase 'with musical notes', or the like.

Earlier published catalogues subsumed into the *Catalogue of Printed Music*

The *Catalogue of Printed Music in the British Library to 1980* includes the contents of a number of earlier published catalogues. What follows gives their titles and summary contents, outlines the circumstances of their publication, and also relates the acquisition of the Paul Hirsch Music Library and the Royal Music Library to their respective catalogues.

The first catalogue issued by the British Museum was:
Catalogue of Printed Music published between 1487 and 1800 now in the British Museum. By W. Barclay Squire. vol.I pp.iv.775; vol.II pp.719. 1912.
Vol.II includes the first supplement.

For the origins and full history of this catalogue, see King, *Printed Music in the British Museum* (pp.139ff.). The Squire catalogue included important works of musical theory (omitted in *CPM*) as well as practical music. It was primarily a composer catalogue, and included the usual cross-references from the titles of vocal works. There were also generic headings for various kinds of anthologies, such as CHANSONS, MOTETS, COUNTRY DANCES and the like. Larger composer headings, such as Haydn, Dibdin and Mozart, were supplied with title indexes of vocal pieces. The sheets of the Squire catalogue were cut up and laid down to form folio volumes, as the basis of the two working copies of a catalogue of pre-1801 music for use within the British Museum. In the course of time many of the original pressmarks were altered.

Squire's catalogue was followed by:

Catalogue of Printed Music published before 1801 now in the British Museum. Second supplement. By William C. Smith. pp.85. 1940.

This catalogue was constructed on the same lines as its predecessor. (For its origins and contents, see King *op. cit.* pp.146-7.) The entries were cut up and incorporated into the laid-down copies of the Squire catalogue.

In 1911 King George V deposited on loan in the British Museum the royal collection of music, which was presented outright to the Trustees in 1957 by Queen Elizabeth II, to mark the bicentenary of the gift of the Old Royal Library. The collection was first known as the 'King's Music Library' and later as the 'Royal Music Library'. The latter designation tallies with the first component of all its pressmarks, 'R.M.'. (The catalogue was published in three volumes, of which the first two comprise manuscripts, and are listed below on p.12, where manuscripts added subsequently are also mentioned.) The third volume is:

British Museum. Catalogue of the King's Music Library. By William Barclay Squire. Part III. Printed Music and Musical Literature. [Completed by William C. Smith.] pp.x.277. 1929.

The musical literature was included in the third edition of the *General Catalogue of Printed Books*, and the music in *CPM.*

In 1946 the British Museum, with the aid of special grants from the Treasury and the Pilgrim Trust, purchased for £120,000 the Hirsch Music Library. It had been built up by

Paul Hirsch (b.1881) at Frankfurt on the Main from about 1898 onwards, and was removed to Cambridge, England, in 1936. This library comprised both music and musical literature. Hirsch himself had issued the following catalogues:

Katalog einer Mozart-Bibliothek. Zu W. A. Mozarts 150. Geburtstag 27. Januar 1906. [By Paul Hirsch.] pp.75. Druck von Wüsten & Schönfeld: Frankfurt A.M., 1906.

This represented an early stage of Hirsch's lifelong special interest in music.

Subsequently Hirsch issued catalogues of the most important part of his entire collection, finely printed, and supplied with full bibliographical descriptions:

Katalog der Musikbibliothek Paul Hirsch Frankfurt am Main. Herausgegeben Kathi Meyer und Paul Hirsch.

Bd. I. Theoretische Drucke bis 1800. pp.299. pl.XXX. Martin Breslauer: Berlin, 1928.

Bd.II. Opern-Partituren. pp.331. pl.XXXI. Martin Breslauer: Berlin, 1930.

Bd.III. Instrumental- und Vokalmusik bis etwa 1830. pp.361. pl.XXXI. Frankfurt am Main, 1936.

Bd.IV. Erstausgeben, Chorwerke in Partitur, Gesamtausgaben, Nachschlagewerke, etc. Ergänzungen zu Bd.I-III. pp.xxiii. 692. pl.XXXVI. University Press: Cambridge, 1947.

Bd.IV includes comprehensive indexes to the entire publication.

Hirsch acquired far more books on music than he could include in Bd.I and Bd.IV above: their treatment for ultimate inclusion in the British Museum's *General Catalogue*, is described on p.42. Hirsch also accumulated much important music which had only been listed in his private card catalogue, and which ranged beyond the categories and dates that he set as limits for inclusion in his four-volume published catalogue. In order, therefore, to have all the music entered in the Museum's music catalogue, the musical works in Bd.II, III and IV above were re-catalogued, according to the BM rules, to form a special Accessions Part. The resultant publication was:

Catalogue of Printed Music in the British Museum. Accession Part 53. Music in the Hirsch library. pp.438. 1951.

It should be mentioned that this Accession Part also includes numerous items which Hirsch purchased from 1946 up to the time of his death in 1951 and generously presented to his former library.

The entries in the Accessions Part conform to the relatively simple style used in the music catalogue. For additional bibliographical and descriptive details of many kinds, Hirsch's own catalogues remain indispensable.

Literature

Anon, 'A £120,000 Music Library for the British Museum', *Illustrated London News*, 13 July 1946, 52-3.

[Dent, Edward J.] 'The Hirsch Library [a review of vol.IV of the catalogue]', *Times Literary Supplement*, 13 March 1948.

King, A. H., 'The Hirsch Music Library', *British Museum Quarterly*, XV, 1952, 11-13.

King, A. H., 'The Hirsch Music Library – retrospect and conclusion', *Notes*, XI, 1952, 381-7.

King, A. H., 'Paul Hirsch and his Music Library', *British Library Journal*, 7, 1981, 1-11.

King, A. H., 'A Swiss Account of Mozart in 1766 [by Samuel Tissot, in *Aristide ou le citoyen*, a copy given by Hirsch to his former library in 1950]', *British Museum Quarterly*, XVI, 1952, 59-60.

Muir, Percy H., 'The Hirsch Catalogue', *Music Review*, 9, 1948, 102-7.

Some ten years after Paul Hirsch's death in 1951, his widow, Olga Hirsch, presented to the Museum a large collection of papers relating to the library – account books, invoices, a visitors' book dating from its early years at Frankfurt, correspondence with musicians and scholars, programmes of concerts given in his house and much else. There is a typescript index of the various categories and another of the names of the writers of the letters. These papers are now preserved in the Music Library.

Periodicals contain a good deal of music, sometimes entire compositions, sometimes bibliographically important excerpts.

For these, there is:

Handlist of Music published in some British and foreign Periodicals between 1787 and 1848 now in the British Museum. [By Unity Sherrington.] pp.80. 1962.

The entries in this catalogue have been included in the *CPM*.

In 1953 the Madrigal Society deposited its library (it comprises both printed and manuscript music: minute books and other papers were deposited later) on indefinite loan in the British Museum. There was issued:

Printed Music in the Library of the Madrigal Society. An excerpt from Part 59 of the Catalogue of Accessions of Printed Music. 1955.

The manuscripts, which are uncatalogued, are mentioned on pp.35, 36.

Subsidiary, unpublished catalogues

National music

Three volumes folio, comprising duplicates of all those entries from the general catalogue of printed music which are 'national' in character, ie consisting of 'folk' music in the broadest sense of the term. The entries are arranged under countries, in chronological order. This catalogue was first compiled retrospectively in about 1925 by William C. Smith and Charles Humphries, and has since been augmented, up to the end of 1980, by the relevant entries from the annual Accessions Part. It has not been possible to keep the country headings up to date in terms of geographical and political changes. A few headings such as GIPSIES and JEWS are exceptions to the geographical principle. There is also a heading NURSERY RHYMES.

The catalogue of National Music is available in the Music Reading Area. The five following catalogues can be consulted only in the Music Library itself, and all are on cards, except that of the Song Albums, which is on manuscript slips. The approximate number of cards in each catalogue is given in round brackets.

1 ***Regimental marches***

An index of British regimental marches arranged in five main categories – 1 Mounted regiments. 2 Foot guards. 3 Foot regiments. 4 Corps. 5 Militia, volunteers and territorials. There are also smaller sections for the Royal Navy, the Royal Marines and the Royal Air Force. A final section gives historical references. (600)

2 ***Pre-1801 music***
Comprises the main entries from Squire's 1912 catalogue and those of Smith's 1940 supplement, cut up and mounted on cards and classified by broad categories. No additions have been made since 1940. (20,000)

3 ***Post-1800 instrumental music***
Entries extracted selectively from the Accession Parts, 1884 to c.1963, broadly classified by forms, groups of instruments and solo instruments. A section devoted to tutors and methods for about 100 different instruments includes some post-1963 entries, and in addition, for the sake of convenience, the cards for the pre-1800 imprints in this category. There is also a section of some 300 vocal tutors. (80,000)

4 ***Song albums***
An index to some 75 English albums and anthologies, some issued periodically, of popular songs – comic, music-hall, coon and minstrel, and the like – published mostly in London from 1870 to c.1955. The slips are arranged alphabetically under the full title of each song, followed by the name(s) of the composer(s) and the title of the album abridged to its initial letters. There is available a typescript list which collates the initials with the full title of each album and gives its pressmark. (12,000)

5 ***Dance notation***
An index of music which includes a visual representation of the steps of the dances.

Classical settings
There is a MS slip index of musical settings, mostly in the collections of the Music Library, of poems – both in the originals and in translation – by Horace, Anacreon, Sappho and other poets. The index was compiled by Sir Henry Thomas, Principal Keeper of Printed Books, 1943-48, and an amateur singer. With the index is a copy of a paper, 'Musical

settings of Horace's lyric poems', which Thomas read to the (Royal) Musical Association, session 46, 1919-20. Pressmark: K.6.d.1.

Index of uncatalogued 'secondary' vocal music, etc.

As mentioned above, *CPM* does not include entries for all the works that have been received by copyright. All such vocal and instrumental music received before 1909 has been fully catalogued and the entries have been duly incorporated. But owing to lack of staff, music received by copyright since those dates has necessarily been catalogued selectively, and a very large number of pieces which had to be deemed as of 'secondary' importance has not been catalogued. This category includes popular songs, dance music of various kinds, band parts, certain educational works for piano, and the like. All 'secondary' music has, however, been treated in such a way that it is available on request. This may be explained in some detail.

It is not bound, but is stored in two series of parcels, one for instrumental works, the other for vocal. In each series the music is grouped into sequences of ten years – 1920-29, 1930-39, and so on – and the pieces are filed alphabetically under the name of the composer, anonymous publications being grouped at the end of the alphabetical sequence for each decade. For the vocal music, a manuscript slip index has been maintained: it is arranged under the title of the piece, which stands first. Then follow the name of the composer and the date of copyright receipt. A typed copy of this slip index, preserved in sheaf binders, comprises entries for 'secondary' music received up to the end of 1949, and is available in the Music Reading Area. For secondary vocal music published since then, the up-to-date slip index kept in the Music Library may be consulted on request.

This system was devised to provide a simple way of making the 'secondary' music available. For vocal works, the title was used as the primary factor in the index because it was found by experience that as the composer's name was often not known, the title was likely to be the cardinal point of any enquiry. The system also ensured that 'secondary' music by any composer could easily be found in bulk, whether or not the titles were a significant part of the enquiry. For instrumental music, however, no slip index of titles was created, largely because the name of the composer was generally known by the enquirer, the title being of less importance. Consequently the alphabetical arrangement under those names, as described above, proved sufficient.

Catalogues, etc. of manuscripts forming part of the Music Library

The manuscripts in the Royal Music Library have been preserved together with the printed music (see p.6), and are catalogued in the following volumes:

British Museum. Catalogue of the King's Music Library. By William Barclay Squire.

Part I. The Handel Manuscripts. [By W. B. Squire.] pp.xi. 143. 1927.

Part II. The miscellaneous Manuscripts. By Hilda Andrews. pp.x. 277. 1929.

In 1926 there was added to the royal music a collection of over eighty volumes transferred from the Chapel Royal, St James's. This comprised English church music dating from the last quarter of the seventeenth century up to about 1850. Another five volumes, consisting of string accompaniments (one for lute, four for violoncello), came to light in 1968, in the Chapel Royal, St James's, and were added by permission to the previous collection. A card index to these manuscripts is available. It is in two sections, comprising: (1) a title index of anthems, referring to the composers; (2) a composer index, giving the works written by each and the names of the extant parts, with the pressmarks. (c.1600 cards). For a description of the collection, see the article by Margaret Laurie (p.13).

There are about seventy-five manuscripts in the Hirsch Library, which are to be found under various headings in the four-volume catalogue. They are also included in Pamela Willetts's *Handlist of Music Manuscripts acquired 1908-67* ('Music Room manuscripts', pp.86-98).

Manuscripts bound up with printed music, or forming

part of a collection of it, are to be found in the categorized lists at the beginning of each volume of the Hughes-Hughes catalogue (see p.62) and in the Willetts *Handlist* (as above).

There is no catalogue of the manuscripts in the library of the Madrigal Society.

Literature

For manuscripts in the Royal Music Library in general, see:
A. H. King, *Some British Collectors of Music, etc.* Cambridge University Press, Cambridge, 1963, pp.103-29, Appendix A, 'The Royal Music Library and its collectors'.

Bray, Roger, 'British Museum MS Royal 24.d.2. An index and a commentary [to John Baldwin's commonplace book]', *Royal Musical Association Research Chronicle*, 12, 1974, 137-51.

King, A. H., *Handel and his Autographs*, pp.32, pl.XX. 1967, repr. 1979.

Laurie, Margaret, 'The Chapel Royal Partbooks', *Music and bibliography. Essays in honour of Alec Hyatt King.* Edited by Oliver Neighbour, Saur/Bingley: London, New York, 1980, pp.28-50.

Neighbour, O. W., 'An unknown Mendelssohn Autograph [a letter of 1844, bound in one of two volumes of music for piano duet, once part of the Royal Music Library, and now restored to it]', *British Library Journal*, 4, 1978, 200.

Squire, W. Barclay, 'Handel's Clock Music [on pieces in R.M.18.b.18 and R.M.19.a.1, composed for a musical clock made by Charles Clay]', *Musical Quarterly*, V, 1919, 538-52.

THE SCOPE OF THE COLLECTIONS

Printed music

The purpose of this section is to give some idea of the interest, character and variety of these collections. For convenience, the music is treated in two main groups – national (including works by foreign composers published in England) and international.

From the late 1820s onwards, when the Trustees first adopted a systematic policy for the development of the Department of Printed Books, they realized that music should receive its due, with special attention paid to music by British composers. The continual pursuit of this policy gradually bore fruit in a comprehensive collection dating back to the second decade of the sixteenth century when printed mensural music began to appear in England. (Although plain-song in service books was printed earlier, it is not discussed here because, as already mentioned, such books, English and foreign, are entered not in the music catalogue, but only in the *General Catalogue of Printed Books*, under the heading LITURGIES.)

Compared with Europe, England was late in this field, but it had the distinction of producing, as its first extant piece of mensural music, what is also the earliest of all broad-sides with notes – the fragmentary ballad 'Away mornynge', which John Rastell printed about 1520. Rastell also issued the earliest known music printed – however roughly – in score, a part-song, 'Tyme to pas'. It is found in his own play *The Interlude of the Four Elements*, which probably dates from about 1525. (These two pieces also provide the first known examples of the use of moveable type to print words and music at a single impression.) Together with the superbly printed bassus part, the only complete one extant, of the *xx Songes* of 1530 (the work of an unidentified London printer), Rastell's pieces form a notable foundation for secular music in the collections.

In the mid-sixteenth century appeared some important books of church music. One of the rarest in the collections is the first issue of *The Actes of the Apostles, translated into English Metre, with Notes to eche Chapter, to synge and also to play upon the Lute*, by Christopher Tye (1553). Soon after, there begins the long sequence of English editions of the psalms set to music, which are entered under that heading in the music catalogue. In 1562 John Day issued the first of many editions in which the melodies are set to the metrical version of Thomas Sternhold and John Hopkins. Day was also responsible for two other landmarks of Protestant church music – *Certaine Notes set forth in foure and three parts* (1560) and *Mornyng and Evenynge Prayer* (1565). In 1575 Thomas Vautrollier printed the famous *Cantiones sacrae* of Thomas Tallis and William Byrd. The latter's Masses, of three, four and five parts, all c.1588, and his other sacred compositions, are all in the Music Library.

At the same time, there dawned the great age of the Elizabethan part-song and madrigal, which lasted well into the next century. The collections are very rich in these works, all issued in parts, by such masters as Byrd, Whythorne, Weelkes, Morley, East, Orlando Gibbons, Vautor, and many others. The first appearance of Scottish music of this type is the cantus part (the sole issued) of John Forbes's *Songs and Fancies* (1666).

No less important, and equally well represented, is the instrumental music of that period, such as Antony Holborne's *Pavans, Galliards . . . in five Parts for Viols, Violins, or other musical wind Instruments* (1595), Thomas Robinson's two instruction books, *New Citharen Lessons* (1609) and *The Schoole of Musicke* (1603), and the *Fantasies of three Parts* of Orlando Gibbons (c.1620). Another landmark is *Parthenia or the Maydenheade of the first Musicke that ever was printed for the Virginalls*, of which the library has the second issue, of c.1615, and two later editions. Another group comprises the lute songs by such masters as Dowland, Campion, often elegantly printed – after the style of manuscripts – in the format of a 'table-book', in which the several parts are disposed on two open pages, so as to face performers seated at different sides of a table. Some other rare lute songs in the collections are Philip Rosseter's *Booke of Ayres* (1601) and Coprario's *Funeral Teares. For the death of the Right Honorable the Earle of Devonshire* (1606).

From the period just before the Civil War, the General Library has an unusual book by one William Barriffe, entitled: *Mars, his Triumphe: Or, the description of the exercise performed the xviii. of October 1638, in the Merchant-Taylors Hall by certain Gentlemen of the Artillery Garden, London* (1639), which is of interest because it contains the music of three marches, perhaps the earliest printed in England. Church music of this era is generously represented, by such famous publications as William Childe's delicately engraved *Psalms* of 1639, John Barnard's *First Book of selected Church Musick* (1641), a very important collection superbly printed in a unique *civilité* type, and *Musica deo sacra* by Thomas Tomkins (1668), So many books of English psalms (other than Sternhold and Hopkins) and hymns were published from the late seventeenth century onwards, that despite numerous purchases, there have always been lacunae. All the more welcome, therefore, was a gift received in 1949 from Church House, Westminster, which presented to the British Museum its entire library. As it included some 1200 books of psalms and hymns with music, many of great rarity, it filled many gaps, especially in the English collections. The two most noteworthy groups were the eighteenth century books amassed and annotated by A. H. Mann, organist of King's College, Cambridge, and numerous nineteenth century publications marked 'Horder Collection'. (These books are now mainly placed at A.1230, B.1172-77, C.15-22, F.1120-23.)

Even during the Protectorate secular music flourished. *The English Dancing Master* (later entitled *The Dancing Master*) began its long career in 1651, and was to reach its eighteenth edition in 1728; most of these editions are in the collections. Secular music, both vocal and instrumental, was fostered by the far-sighted publisher John Playford (the initiator of *The Dancing Master*), whose numerous anthologies and instruction books are among the library's treasures from the middle of the seventeenth century. They include *Select musicall Ayres* (1652), *Musick's Recreation on the Lyra Viol* (1652), *Musick's Delight on the Cithren* (1666), and *Musick's Hand-maid: presenting new and pleasant Lessons and Instructions for the Virginals or Harpsycon* (1663). Playford's son, Henry, published among other important anthologies *The Theater of Music* (1685-7), a collection of songs 'sung at the court, and public theaters'. Some of the library's copies of John Playford's publications are unique. Another *unicum* of this period is Richard Mathew's *The Lute's Apology for her Excellency* (1652), the only English lute book issued between 1610 and 1676. Mathew catered for much the same public as John Playford. The collections include fine music by various immigrant composers of this time, such as *Songs set by Pietro Reggio* (1680).

The later part of this century saw the emergence of Purcell as a native composer of genius, followed in the next generation by Handel, who became a British subject in 1727. Both were very prolific, and the Music Library's holding of the numerous editions of their works is perhaps the most comprehensive in the world. Among Handel editions it is noteworthy that there are the first four issues of *Songs in Messiah*. It was during and just after Handel's time that London became increasingly one of the great international music-publishing centres of Europe. Consequently, it later proved desirable for the Music Library to acquire retrospectively English editions not only of British composers, but also of European music printed in this country. Thus, the holding of Handel's music is matched by that of London editions of his Italian contemporaries such as Locatelli, Corelli, Tartini, Vivaldi and Bononcini.

Various pieces by lesser composers from this period were later fathered on to the great names, one of the most notorious being 'Purcell's' Trumpet Voluntary which became widely popular in various arrangements during and just after the Second World War. The original was in fact a little tune by Jeremiah Clarke (c.1674-1707), which appears under his name, with the title 'The Prince of Denmark's March', in *A Choice Collection of Ayres for the Harpsichord . . . by John Blow* [and others] (1700), of which the library has the unique copy.

A peculiarly British type of music — the folio single-sheet song printed from an engraved plate — became very popular from the 1690s onwards. Throughout the eighteenth century a vast quantity was issued, principally in London, but also, as time wore on, in Edinburgh, and in Dublin where the English ones were often reprinted. The music was by an extraordinary variety of composers, famous and obscure, and often included, at the foot of the sheet, a version for flute or guitar. Probably by far the largest single assemblage of these songs is that in the Music Library, which runs to several thousand, including the remarkable collection made by Charles Burney, which was purchased by the British Museum in 1838. The texts cover an extensive range of topics, from love-songs and pastoral scenes to social and political satire.

The eighteenth century was notable not only for the quantity of music published in England, but also for its variety. Dancing, for instance, became a national passion, expanded enormously from the time and range of *The Dancing Master*, mentioned above. Court dances, by such popular instructors as L'Abbé, Pemberton, Isaac, and Kellom Tomlinson, and country dances became all the rage, and were published in large quantities, both in collections and singly, all well represented in the collections. Such dances even appeared on playing cards – one set of c.1725, still in its original woven case, is in the Hirsch Library (IV. 1444) – and on fans (see pp.138-9). Minuets too were very popular, and are to be found in the music catalogue under that generic title. The need of amateurs for self-tuition is reflected in the numerous 'tutors' or 'instructions' for various instruments. (Mostly anonymous, they are entered under those headings in the catalogue.) A type of publication much favoured in eighteenth century England (as also, to a lesser extent, in France and Germany) was the illustrated songbook. The music library has a score or so of them, issued in folio, such as George Bickham's *Musical Entertainer* (1737,38), in quarto, like *Amaryllis* (1746) and *Universal Harmony* (1745), or in octavo, like *Clio and Euterpe* (1748-62). Most are printed on fine paper with elegant headpieces or vignettes to each page, illustrating the topic of the song. From this period begins the outpouring of songs for the pleasure gardens at Vauxhall, by such prolific composers as Thomas Augustine Arne, Worgan and Hook, all numerous in the collections.

Male voice part-singing flourished at this time as never before, even in Purcell's day. To meet this need, which developed until well into the nineteenth century, some bulky collections of glees and catches, such as those made by E. T. Warren, were issued. Other examples of this type of music are the printed works preserved in the library of the Madrigal Society, the collections of the Abbey Glee Club (now placed at E.205 a-q, and H.1202 a-ii), and of the Noblemen and Gentlemen's Catch Club (E.1858, E.1858 a-z, aa-dd, H.2788, H.2788 a-z, aa-zz, aaa-ggg).

While catch and glee flourished, instrumental music grew equally in popularity. The great demand for symphonies, concertos and quartets is seen in a comprehensive array of such compositions by Stanley, Arne, Boyce, Avison, J. C. Bach and Storace, and in editions of similar works by foreign musicians who became popular in England – Cambini, Antonio Kammel, Carl Stamitz, Carlo Tessarini, Francesco Zannetti and many others. Keyboard music of the later eighteenth century reached its apogee in the sonatas by Haydn which were published in London during his two visits in the 1790s. From the next generation, there are numerous editions of Clementi's rondos, sonatas and variations, and similar pieces by Dussek. Opera and other kinds of theatrical entertainments with music, so widely popular at this time, are fully represented in the works of such prolific composers as Shield, Dibdin, Kelly, Storace and Reeve, to name but a few.

By far the largest part of the music so far mentioned was purchased in fulfilment of the policy that the British Museum should have the most complete collection possible of what was published in Great Britain. It is true that some English music, published from about 1760 onwards, did find its way into the British Museum through Stationers' Hall, and so slightly reduced the quantity which posterity had to acquire by purchase. But it was only the tip of an ever-growing iceberg. It might also be expected that the strict requirements of successive Copyright Acts, especially those of 1814 and 1842, would have adeed to the desired degree of completeness, but unfortunately this was not so. Many music publishers, particularly some of the larger ones in London, ignored the Acts, or only fulfilled their requirements very irregularly. They deliberately risked prosecution because they knew that the British Museum would only pursue its rights in the courts very selectively and intermittently. Many other firms, even the smaller ones in London, and – perhaps understandably – those in the remoter parts of the country, remained quite unaware of their obligations under the Acts. The proportion of music deposited was only a tiny fraction of what was published. (In this context, it is worth remembering that during the nineteenth century London became the most prolific centre of music publishing in Europe, second, perhaps, only to Paris.)

Nevertheless, copyright did secure for the British Museum some very important pieces – many London editions of Beethoven, contemporaneous with the composer, some of which were 'authentic' (ie printed with his sanction) while others were 'unauthentic'.

In the field of ballet, there are piano scores of many works of Cesare Bossi, the Italian composer popular in London at the turn of the century. A little later, copyright brought in many first English editions of Chopin and Mendelssohn, some published simultaneously with those issued abroad. Again, there is a fine assemblage from copyright of the English first editions of Dvořák. But for an English composer of an earlier generation, such as William Crotch, many works had to be purchased. Even more did this apply to the innumerable editions and arrangements of Haydn and Mozart which were reprinted in London from foreign originals. But by about 1880, deposit began to become more regular, at least by the larger publishers.

The range of music by English musicians of the nineteenth century is enormous. The collections include the church music of the Wesleys, the songs of Edward Loder, the large and very varied output of Macfarren and Sterndale Bennett, and the operettas of Sullivan. Virtuoso and educational piano pieces, ranging from the serious studies of J. B. Cramer to the glittering trifles of Sidney Smith, are here in abundance, as are collections of psalms and hymns. Besides all these and their like, the Copyright Act secured English editions of the three most popular Italian opera composers of the age – Bellini, Donizetti and Verdi – in a continual stream of vocal scores, extracts and arrangements.

Towards the end of the nineteenth century came the renaissance of English music, beginning with Elgar, Parry, Delius and Vaughan Williams, and continuing into the twentieth with Holst and Britten. Again, copyright brought almost all this wealth of creativity into the collections, although some of Elgar's early works were first published abroad, and had to be acquired by purchase. An occasional rarity escaped the net – for instance, his *May Song* (published with beautiful designs by Walter Crane), of which there was a limited edition of five copies, printed on vellum. (Fortunately, a copy of this rarity was in the Hirsch Library.)

There is one collection of romantic music by English composers, of a rather unusual character. It consists of proof sheets of works published by the London house of Augener, in the early decades of the twentieth century (pressmark H.403 a-z, aa-zz). The composers include Ireland, Warlock, Frank Bridge, Butterworth, Holst and Delius. Of the last named, only a few of the proof sheets are corrected by him: in the majority of the works the corrections are in the hand either of his wife Jelka or of his friend Philip Heseltine. This collection, which also includes some proof corrections by a few European composers such as Reger, is interesting as affording a glimpse of various methods of work during the penultimate stage of production.

It is a far cry from the romantics to the music of the so-called 'avant-garde' – such as the works of Cornelius Cardew, the electronic music of Roger Smalley, and the immensely complex scores of Brian Ferneyhough: here too copyright deposit has enriched the collections.

Another example of the weakness of that Act is the large quantity of Welsh hymns, psalms, choral works and part-songs, published from about 1870 onwards, and often printed in tonic sol-fa, which have been purchased retrospectively. Scottish bagpipe music is well represented, as are also songs in Gaelic printed in Dublin. As relics of popular Victorian entertainment, there are many editions of the songs of the Christy Minstrels, and an immense number of music-hall songs, which – up to the First World War – were often published with handsome chromolithographed title-pages (see also (p.34), now of considerable social and artistic interest. Similar title-pages are found on quadrilles and other dances composed for domestic use and based, for instance, on the ever-popular music of Sullivan and Offenbach. At contrasting ends of the social scale are the collections of songs or the single songs composed for the English public schools, such as those edited for Harrow by John Farmer, and the *Eton Boating Song* (1878) (of which one or two extraordinary instrumental arrangements were published), and all the albums of songs composed by the 'Beatles' and their lesser rivals and successors – all these secured for posterity by copyright deposit.

It should be remembered that the foregoing account of music published in the British Isles during the last four and a half centuries is necessarily very selective, and can only offer an outline of the catholicity and variety of this aspect of the collections in the Music Library.

Catholicity, in the widest sense of the word, is the essence of the holdings of music composed in the western tradition and printed outside the United Kingdom, which means – broadly speaking – in Europe, including Russia, and in the Americas. From about 1850 to 1886 International Copyright brought in many editions of French and German works, and more recently a wealth of music from the United States has been deposited by American publishers. Otherwise, acquisitions have largely been by purchase, and were based on a simple but ambitious policy – to attempt to build up a collection of music by all the significant composers of every country, so that it might be the best, for all periods, from the earliest years of music printing onwards, outside the national library of each. With limited funds and staff, complete fulfulment of this policy has not been universally possible. Nevertheless, it has produced, for example, one of the best collections of Finnish music outside Finland, of Italian music outside Italy, and so on. The following selective outline is given in roughly chronological order, and, for the sake of convenience, in groups of broadly the same kind.

Mensural music began to be published in Europe during the last decade of the fifteenth century, as a small adjunct to books of several kinds – a play, a devotional work or a school textbook. Some examples in the collections are: Carolus Verardus, *In historiam Baeticam praefatio* (Rome, 1493), which has a four-part Spanish song *Viva el gran re Fernando*; *Von sant Ursulen schifflin* (issued by the Confraternity of St Ursula, Strassburg, 1497), in which there is a song, *Das liede vber sant Ursulen schyfflin*, perhaps the earliest printed in German, the words by Johannes Gosseler, who possibly also wrote the music; Conradus Celtes, *Ludus Diane in modum comedie* (Nuremberg, 1500), with the music of two choruses. Such were the precursors of the first books of music, both sacred and secular, which were issued by Ottaviano Petrucci of Venice from 1501 onwards. A volume of motets dated 1503 is the earliest in the British Library, which has a dozen more issued by the same printer before 1520. Besides anthologies, these important rarities include volumes of masses by single composers, such as Fevin, Colin, Isaac, Pierre de la Rue and Josquin des Près. The collections are rich in other fine anthologies – masses issued by Andreas Antico of Rome (1516), motets by Moderne of Paris (1532), by Gardane of Venice (1538 to 1549), by Susato of Antwerp (1546 to 1555) and by Phalèse of Louvain (1555 to 1558).

The collections also contain some notable volumes of sacred music each by a single composer – Cardinal Francisco Ximenez de Cisneros (editor), *Passionarium toletanum* (Alcala de Henares, 1516); Ludwig Senfl, *Liber selectarum cantionum* (Vienna, 1520); Luther, *Deudsche Messen* (Nuremberg, 1526); Isaac, *Choralis Constantinus* (Nuremberg, 1550-55); Stephanus, a Monk of the Military Order of Christ, *Liber passionum* (Lisbon, 1595). From the later 1580s onwards, the numerous editions of Palestrina's hymns, masses and motets reflect his great popularity. Here may be mentioned two lesser known composers whose works indicate the remarkable range of sacred music in the collections, east and west – two books of Bohemian psalms by Tobiáš Záworka, *Pisnie Chwal Božských* (Prague, 1602) and *Zpjwanj Pohřebnij Store y Nowé* (Prague, 1592), and Juan Navarro's *Liber in quo quattuor Passiones Christi Domini continentur* (Mexico, 1604), the first music composed in the New World. Bestriding this period like a colossus is Orlande de Lassus, of whose works, both secular and sacred, the library has a comprehensive collection in first and contemporary editions, dating from the mid-1550s up to 1610.

Secular vocal music was published in quantity rather later than was instrumental. In France Pierre Attaingnant issued books of chansons from 1527 onwards; the earliest of the sequence in the library dates from 1540. Jacques Moderne's great collection, *Le Parangon des Chansons*, appeared in nine books at Lyons from 1548 to 1541, followed in 1554 by the first of the long series published by Le Roy and Ballard; their last appeared in 1571. Unlike these French publishers, their Italian counterparts devoted themselves to individual musicians rather than to anthologies. These books of madrigals form one of the largest categories of sixteenth century music in the Music Library, including such important composers as Verdelot, Marenzio, Filippo de Monte, Rore, and Wert, to name but a few. A distinctive type of vocal music is found in the canzonette and other songs, secular and sacred, edited by Simone Verovio (Rome, 1586 onwards), some with lute or keyboard accompaniment, and printed from elegantly engraved plates. (This is the earliest substantial use of this process.)

In instrumental music of the sixteenth century, pride of place goes to Marco Antonio Cavazzoni's *Recbercari, motetti, canzoni* (Venice, 1523), one of the two known copies of the earliest printed book of keyboard music. It is complemented by three very rare German books – Sebastian Virdung, *Musica getutscht* (Basle, 1511) an important collection of music in tablature for organ and other instruments, and two by Hans Gerle, *Musica Teusch* (Nuremberg, 1532), and *Tabulatur auff die Laudten* (Nuremberg, 1533). (The latter is unique.) The popularity of the plucked string instrument is shown by the considerable number of tablatures published in several countries.

Five such books for guitar, by Adrian Le Roy (two of them unique in the British Library's copies) appeared in Paris from 1551 to 1554. Another book by him, of which the original is lost, was issued in translation as *A briefe and plaine Instruction to set all Musicke of eight diuers Tunes in Tablature for the Lute* (London, 1574). From other countries, the collections contain such rarities as: Luis de Milan, *Libro de musica de vihuela da mano. Intitulado El maestro* (Valencia, 1536): Luys de Narbaez, *El primero (-sesto) libro del Delphin de musica de cifras para tañer vihuela* (Valladolid, 1538); Francesco da Milano, *Intabolatura de lauto* (books 1,2,3 and 7, Venice, 1546, 1562, 1548); *Carmina pro testudine liber IIII* (Louvain, 1546); Melchior Neusidler, *Intabolatura di liuto* (2 books, Venice, 1566); *Selectissimorum pro testudine carminum liber primus* (Louvain, 1573).

Some more important organ music was issued in the later

part of this century – Bernhard Schmid, *Zwey Bücher. Einer neuen kunstlichen Tabulatur auff Orgel vnd Instrument* (Strassburg, 1577); Jacob Paix, *Ein schön nutz vnnd gebreuchlich Orgel-Tabulaturbuch* (Laugingen, 1583): Johann Woltz *Nova musices organicae tabulatura* (Basle, 1617) are some of the library's riches.

From the early seventeenth century onwards, vocal music, both secular and sacred, flourished in Germany. The collections are rich in the part-books of music by such composers as Michael Praetorius, Johann Crueger, Andreas Hammerschmidt and Melchior Franck. Of the north German composer and poet Heinrich Albert there are eight books of his popular *Arien* (Königsberg, 1638-57). One of the few Danish publications of the early seventeenth century is the two books of madrigals collected by Melchior Borchgrewinck, *Giardino novo bellissimo di varii fiori musicali* (Copenhagen, 1605,06). The enduring popularity of lute and guitar music is shown by three works of Francesco Corbetta, *Varii capricii per la ghitarra spagnuola* (Milan, 1643); *Varii scherzi di sonate per la chitarra spagnola* (Brussels, 1648); *La guitarre royale* (Paris, 1671) and two of Nicolas Vallet, *Paradisus musicus testudinis* (Amsterdam, 1618), and *Le second livre de tabulature de luth, intitulé Le secret des muses* (Amsterdam, 1619).

Late in the sixteenth century and early in the seventeenth, ballet became established as an art form combining dance and music, seen in some fine dance books preserved in the library. The first and in some respects the most sumptuous is Baltasar de Beaujoyeulx, *Balet comique de la royne* (Paris, 1582) illustrated with superbly engraved plates, with the airs printed. Two books by Fabritio Caroso, *Nobiltà di dame* (Venice, 1600) and *Il ballarino* (Venice, 1581), both have beautifully engraved plates by Giacomo Francho (important for the history of the dance and of costume), with the music in lute tabulature to each dance. A similarly elegant style of production is found in Cesare Negri, *Inventioni di balli* (Milan, 1604), with fifty-eight plates of court dances, and with the music as in Caroso's books.

Of the various Italian madrigal composers who flourished at this time Monteverdi is the most famous, and his madrigals up to book 7 are in the Music Library, in various editions, together with his *Scherzi musicali* of 1609. It was during this time that the new art form of opera took shape, represented here by the first and second editions of Jacopo Peri's *Le musiche sopra l'Euridice del Sig. Ottavio Rinuccini* (Florence, 1600 and Venice, 1608), and the second edition of Monteverdi's *L'Orfeo* (Venice, 1615). From the younger generation of operatic composers are two works by Stefano Landi, *La morte d'Orfeo* (Venice, 1619) and *Il S. Alessio* (Rome, 1635), and one by Michel Angelo Rossi, *Erminia sul Giordano* (Rome, 1637), a copy with five sumptuous engravings of scenes in the opera, by F. Greuter after A. Camasso.

For the period that marks the rise of opera in France, the Music Library has a comprehensive collection of the works of Lulli, printed from the 1680s until well into the next century, and amplified in the next generation by the operas and opera-ballets of Campra and the operas of Rameau. Two rare German operas of the early eighteenth century are Reinhard Keyser's *La forza della virtù* and *L'inganno fedele*, both printed, in selected arias, at Hamburg in 1701 and 1714 respectively.

In the field of German keyboard music several notable books appeared at the end of the seventeenth century. The two volumes of Johann Kuhnau's *Neuer Clavier Ubung ersten (andrer) Theil* (Leipzig, 1689,1696) are complemented by Georg Muffat's *Apparatus musico-organisticus* (Vienna, 1690) and Johann Pachelbel's *Hexachordum Apollinis* (Nuremberg, 1699).

One of the most notable groups in the whole collection comprises nearly all the scarce editions of J. S. Bach that were printed in his lifetime. Beginning with his first published work, Cantata no.71, entitled *Glück-wünschende Kirchen Motetto* (Mühlhausen, 1708), it includes all four parts of the *Clavier-Übung* (1727 to 1742) – some copies with the composer's own manuscript corrections – the first part of the *Musicalisches Opfer* (1747), the *Canonic Variations* on *Von Himmel hoch da komm ich her* of 1748, and the *Sechs Chorale von verschiedener Art* of the same year. Of the posthumous publications of Bach perhaps the most notable is the first complete edition of the 'Forty-Eight', issued by

Nägeli of Zürich in 1801. (Among numerous later editions of this work, one curiosity deserves mention here — a selection of eight fugues, edited by Bernhard Boekelmann, Leipzig, 1895, with the subjects in each ingeniously printed in different colours.)

Bach's son Carl Philipp Emanuel was extensively published in his lifetime. One of the most interesting of the numerous first and early editions in the library is a copy of the *VI sonates pour clavecin avec des reprises variées* (Berlin, 1760) which has manuscript variants added, in the composer's hand, to sonatas 3, 4 and 5. By far the most prolific of J. S. Bach's European contemporaries was G. P. Telemann, of whose huge output only a tiny quantity was printed in his lifetime, mostly in editions which are now very scarce. The music library has a score of them, including fifty-three out of the very rare collection of seventy-two church cantatas (Hermsdorff, 1748-49); the single cantata *Du Tochter Zion, freue dich* (Hermsdorff, c.1735); *Harmonischer Gottes-Dienst* (Hamburg, 1725) and *Fortsetzung des Harmonischen Gottes-Dienstes* (Hamburg, 1731); the vocal score of *Music von Leiden und Sterben des Welt Erlösers* (Nuremberg, c.1745); *Fantaisies pour le clavessin; 3. douzaines* (c.1740) and *Fugues legères & petits jeux, a clavessin seul* (Hamburg, c.1730). These last two books of harpsichord music are balanced in the collections by their very important French counterparts — François Couperin's *Pièces de clavecin, livres 1 — 4* (Paris, 1713 to 1730) and Rameau's *Pièces de clavessin* (Paris, 1724) and *Nouvelles pièces de clavecin* (Paris, c.1735).

From this period date some notable song-books and dance-books, mostly printed from engraved plates. Outstanding is Gregorio Lambranzi, *Neue und curieuse Theatrialische Tantz-Schul* (Nuremberg, 1716), in which the engraving of the dancers and the music, done by J. G. Puschner, is of almost the same quality as in the Italian books (see p.25) of the preceding century. The works of R. A. Feuillet, *Recueil de contredances mises en choreographie* (Paris, 1706) and *Recueil de dances* (Paris, 1700) show each dance accompanied by the delicate pattern of the steps. (The collections also contain his theoretical works on the dance, in the original French and in English translation.) A splendid group of

German song-books is that by 'Sperontes' (the pseudonym of Johann Sigismund Scholze), all entitled *Sperontes Singende Muse an der Pleisse*, and published at Leipzig in various editions and continuations between 1736 and 1747. In each book the finely engraved music at the head of the page is complemented by small woodcuts of musical figures and other charming decorations set with the columns of the printed text. Even more elaborate is J. B. de Laborde's *Choix de chansons* (4 vol., Paris, 1773). The numerous full-page illustrations, designed by J. M. Moreau le jeune, and engraved by Moria and Madame Vendôme, are of the highest quality. Each picture mirrors the words of the song printed opposite – a perfect reflection of the society and manners of the age. The collections include three rare unillustrated Russian song-books – J. G. Prach, *Sobranie narodnykh russkikh pesen s ikh golossami* (St. Petersburg, 1790), V. T. Trutovsky, *Sobranie russkikh prostich s notamye* (St. Petersburg, 1782,78,89, 3 vol., and a third edition, 4 vol., 1796,78-95), and *Pesennik' ili polnoye sobranie* (anonymous, St. Petersburg, 1796?, vol. 1 only: 3 vol. 1798?).

The collections contain a wealth of later instrumental tutors and instruction books, published in many European countries from the end of the seventeenth century onwards. The following is a small selection, some familiar, others perhaps not. One of the best known keyboard books is C. P. E. Bach's *Versuch über die wahre Art das Clavier zu spielen*, of which there are the first and second editions of each of the two parts and a third edition of the first part. spanning the years 1753 to 1787. Among violin methods Leopold Mozart's *Versuch einer gründlichen Violinschule* is found in the first edition (1756), a Dutch translation (1766), followed by other texts in French (1770 and c.1805), German (1806 and 1817), English (an abridgement, 1812?), up to musical excerpts issued in Hungary in 1965. This is a remarkable testimony to the originality of its author's mind, which led to a longevity of over two centuries – something enjoyed by few of his successors, even Pierre Baillot's *L'art du violon: nouvelle methode*, (1834).

For the hurdy-gurdy there are the *Traité de la musette* (1672) of Pierre Borjon de Scellery, a lawyer and man of letters, and François Bouin's *La vielleuse habile* (1770). Among instruction books for guitar may be mentioned Michel Corrette's *Les dons d'Apollon* (1762), and, for the lute, *Livre de musique pour lut* (1680) by — Perrine. Of books for other plucked instruments the numerous holding includes F. V. Corbelin, *Méthode de harpe* (1779) and Pietro Denis, *Méthode pour apprendre à jouer de la mandoline* (c.1780). The Music Library has, among a quantity of flute tutors, the first three editions (1752 to 1789) of J. J. Quantz's *Versuch einer Anweisung, die Flöte traversiere zu spielen*, as well as the French version of 1752. The clarinet tutors include J. G. H. Backhofen's *Anweisung zur Klarinette* (1803?).

For brass instruments, there are André Nemetz, *Neueste Posaunschule* (1838), — Hartmann, *Méthode elementaire du saxophone* (1845?), Adolphe Sax, *Méthode complète pour saxhorn et saxotrombe* (1850?), Giuseppe Sianesi, *Metodo per pelittone* (c.1850) – the last being a type of bass tuba named after its inventor Giuseppe Pelitti. Among a quantity of percussion tutors there is C. A. Boracchi, *Manuale per timpanista* (1842). Instruments now obsolete have had their expositors, such as A. Hardy, *Méthode de serpent* (c.1810); J. E. Krähmer, *Neueste theoretisch-praktische Csakan-Schule* – a recorder in the form of a walking stick (c.1825) – J. Wigame, *Méthode d'harmoniflûte* (1850?); F. Funoll y Alpuente, *Metodo completo di bombardino bajo* (1860?), and C. J. Pratten, *Scale and Pieces for the Gigelira* (1882). There are also a few books for oriental instruments, such as Krishnadhan Banerji, *A comprehensive Self-Instructor for the Setar* (1916), though the majority of such publications are kept in the Department of Oriental Manuscripts and Printed Books.

From about the 1760s onwards it is possible to treat rather more summarily other aspects of the collections which are less specialized than most of those mentioned so far. This is because, as both the nature of music changed and the demand became wider, printing grew cheaper and the variety and quantity of publications in the smaller forms increased sharply. The first, and certainly the most important, group of composers to benefit (though not in terms of personal profit) was the so-called Viennese school – Haydn, Mozart, Beethoven and Schubert. The representation of their works in first and early editions is numerous and remarkably comprehensive, thanks in no small measure to the strength of the Hirsch Library.

Of the four masters, Mozart was the only one who had any personal connection with the British Museum. When his father Leopold brought him to visit it in June 1765, he presented to the Trustees copies of the Paris editions of his son's sonatas printed as op.1 and op.2 (K.6-9) and the sonatas published in London as op.3 (K.10-15), with a manuscript motet (see p.38). A further link with the child composer is found in the Royal Music Library – another copy of the sonatas op.3 presented to Queen Charlotte in gratitude for her patronage, with a violin part in Leopold Mozart's hand. Among numerous later editions of Mozart's operas the collections include some that were prepared by eminent conductors. One such is that of the full score of *Idomeneo*, edited by Richard Strauss (Magdeburg, 1931), of which the Library has his conducting copy with expression marks, bowings and additional wind-parts to one aria, all in his hand.

By way of interlude, there are two famous songs which were composed during the 'Viennese' period. One is Claude Joseph Rouget de Lisle's *Chant de guerre pour l'armée du Rhin*, printed at Strasbourg anonymously in 1792, and later known as 'The Marseillaise'. (Besides this, the only copy of the first issue recorded in RISM, the Library also has the first illustrated edition, printed in Paris as a broadside in 1792.) The other is Franz Grüber's *Stille Nacht, heilige Nacht*, which was first printed as one of *Vier ächte Tiroler-Lieder* (Dresden, 1832). From this period there begins the collection of nineteenth century dance-music in which, thanks again largely to Hirsch, the library is very rich. The outstanding names are those of Johann Strauss the elder and the younger, Josef Lanner, and Joseph Labitzky. Many of the first and early editions printed in Vienna, Prague, or Leipzig, are embellished with charming vignettes related to the style of the dance or its place and occasion of performance.

In the early decades of the nineteenth century, the change in the nature of music publishing already mentioned gathered force. With few exceptions, such as full scores of operas and certain types of choral and instrumental compositions, the number of copies printed became much larger and so more survived. Hence they were easier to buy at the time of issue and subsequently. Thus the concept of rarity, which coloured the choice of the music mentioned in the earlier part of this section, now becomes much less relevant, especially as the collections have systematically expanded to reflect the increasingly international character of music. Their scope for the nineteenth and twentieth century need not, then, be enumerated in detail, but can reasonably be indicated in more summary and general terms.

First, however, a few examples of interesting rarities may be mentioned. Among a comprehensive collection of first and early editions of romantic music, one of the choicest pieces is the only known copy (and sole source) of Berlioz's first published work, a song *Le dépit de la bergère* (c.1819-22). Nearly as rare is a song by Verdi *L'Abandonée* (of which also no autograph is known), though the Music Library's copy is not of the first issue. From a different world comes a copy of the extremely scarce first edition of Norbert Schultze's *Lili Marleen* (1940) perhaps the most famous song from the time of the Second World War. As an example of an 'association piece' there is a copy of the two-piano reduction of Tchaikovsky's piano concerto no.1, formerly owned by Edward Dannreuther, who gave the first London performance in 1876. In this copy Dannreuther made copious emendations, which had the composer's approval. An 'association piece' of wider range is the collection of eighty-nine orchestral scores which were owned by Sir John Barbirolli and presented to the Museum in 1971 by his widow (pressmarks: E.1307, etc., G.1503, etc., I.348, etc.). They consist largely of European editions of classical and romantic symphonies, concertos, operas, and the like, all of which bear expression marks and bowings added in Barbirolli's hand. These were the scores that he took with him on his world-wide tours either with the Hallé orchestra or as a guest conductor.

The vast field of western music in the nineteenth and twentieth centuries is fully represented in the Music Library, to take account of the great variety of traditional forms which evolved in the mainstream of romanticism as well as the fluctuating new directions of more recent times. There is, for example, a comprehensive collection of first and early editions of operas in vocal and full score, notably by the composers of the three most prolific and influential schools. The tally of German opera runs from Weber through Marschner and Meyerbeer to Wagner, Berg, Richard Strauss, Fortner and Henze.

Products of the Italian genius crowd the shelves, with works by Rossini and his great contemporaries, followed by Verdi, Boito, Mascagni, Leoncavallo, Cilea, and Puccini, including also many lesser names such as Giulio Cottrau. In succession to French operas by Gluck, Grétry and Dalayrac, the collections are rich in scores by the composers of the revolutionary period such as Méhul, Lesueur and Catel, and a long tradition of others leading to Bizet, Charpentier and Massenet. (Of the last, the Music Library has twenty-five of his operas and other works for the stage in folio full scores). Another generation is represented by such works as Ambroise Thomas' *Hamlet* and *Mignon*, Roussel's scarce choral ballet *Aenéas*, and Poulenc's *Les mamelles de Tirésias*. Countries with a less prolific operatic vein are well represented – Erkel of Hungary, for instance, and Moniuszko of Poland. So too are Janáček and Martinů, in original editions, and the longer Russian tradition from Glinka, Mussorgsky and Rimsky-Korsakov, to Prokofiev and Shostakovich.

The lighter vein of operetta can be comprehensively traced in the collections, from the works of Lortzing, Nicolai and Suppé to those of their successors in the German tradition such as Millöcker and the younger Johann Strauss. (The cosmopolitan Offenbach is also generously represented in numerous first and early editions.) In the next generation of operetta composers (largely Austro-Hungarian), such notable names as Ziehrer, Heuberger, Kálmán, Oscar Straus and Lehár are well covered, and are balanced by their prolific French counterparts, Lecocq and Messager, for example. While most operettas were issued only in vocal score, a few appeared in full orchestral scores, restricted editions usually printed by lithography. Such, in the Music Library, are *Die lustigen Weiber von Windsor* (Nicolai); *Fatiniza, Boccaccio* and *Das Pensionat* (Suppé); *Der Zigeunerbaron, Das Spitzentuch der Königin*, and *Die Fledermaus* (Strauss); *Der Bettelstudent*

(Millöcker); and *Les contes d'Hoffmann* (Offenbach, both the 3-act and the 4-act version). In a rather more exotic field, there is a fair sprinkling of *zarzuelas* by such masters of the genre as Francisco Alonso, Tomás Bretón, Ruperto Chapí, Jacinto Guerrero and Amadeo Vives.

Equally comprehensive is the library's holding of music in other forms, to take account of all the new directions followed by composers from the late nineteenth century onwards – neo-classical, atonal, aleatory, electronic and expressionist. Schönberg, Zemlinsky, Skalkottas, Stravinsky, Webern, Xenakis, Berio, Stockhausen, Globokar, Holliger, Kagel, Barraqué, Rands – such is a sample of the names of the twentieth century to be found in the catalogue. The publication of such developments has often transcended national and geographical boundaries, as may be seen in the series issued by the New Music Society of California (1923 onwards) which includes, besides pieces by American composers, the first edition of Schönberg's *Klavierstück* op.33b (1932). The collections are rich in American music of many kinds, from the traditional style of Parker, Sessions, Copland and the dissonant originality of Ives to the experimental work of Cage and Babbitt.

Thanks, yet again, to the benefits of copyright deposit, popular American music in ample quantity is in the Music Library, by such various masters of their craft as Scott Joplin, Irving Berlin, Victor Herbert, George Gershwin, Duke Ellington, Jerome Kern, Vincent Youmans and Richard Rodgers.

The publications mentioned in the foregoing twenty pages or so have generally been chosen because of their significance as music. Quite a number of them, however, are also interesting because they have finely designed, decorative title-pages, which are of considerable artistic merit. This applies to those printed from woodcut blocks or engraved plates, as well as to those produced later by lithography. While a few of the engraved ones are briefly mentioned in passing in this chapter, the collections contain a very large number of others, of all periods and countries. Even if it were possible to describe them all in this book, it would need a disproportionate amount of space.

But the interested reader may refer to a very useful anthology entirely devoted to such title-pages. It was compiled by Gottfried S. Fraenkel, and is entitled *Decorative Music Title Pages, 201 examples from 1500 to 1800* (Dover Publications; New York, 1968). Fraenkel drew nearly half his examples from copies in the then British Museum collections, which also contain many of those which he reproduced from sources elsewhere. There is likewise Richard Schaal's *Musiktitel aus fünf Jahrhunderten* (Heinrichshofen: Wilhelmshafen, 1972). This shows well over 200 fine title-pages, of which over half are from the nineteenth and twentieth centuries. The majority of these are German, and many will be found in the British Library's collections.

The books by Fraenkel and Schaal are concerned almost exclusively with serious classical music. John Grand-Carteret's *Les titres illustrés et l'image au service de la musique* (Turin, 1904) shows title-pages from their earliest times up to those found in popular European music of his own day. But he largely ignores England. From the early nineteenth century onwards, however, London music publishers issued large quantities of popular songs and piano pieces, a high proportion of which has illustrated title-pages, printed at first in black and white, either by engraving or by lithography, and – after about 1840 – by chromolithography. While only a small number are of high artistic merit, a very large quantity is important for social, theatrical or operatic history. Such title-pages can often be found by serendipity, or through familiarity with the composers' names (eg Charles Handel Marriott and Stephen Glover for popular songs and piano pieces). A more systematic guide, however, is in course of compilation in the Music Library, in the form of a card index arranged according to the subjects of the illustrations: each entry includes the names, when given, of the artist, or printer, or both. This should ultimately form the starting point for a systematic study of this vast field. Selected title-pages are reproduced in such books as Doreen and Sidney Spellman's *Victorian Music Covers* (Evelyn, Adams & Mackay: London, 1969), and Ronald Pearsall's *Victorian Sheet Music*

Covers (David & Charles: Newton Abbott, 1972). One of the masters of the English chromolithographic title-page, Alfred Concanen (1835-86), is the subject of an evocative, illustrated study by Sir Sacheverell Sitwell, *Morning, Noon and Night in London* (Macmillan: London, 1948).

Manuscripts in special collections

With the exception of one category, the manuscripts in the Hirsch Music Library (important as some are in themselves) were peripheral to Hirsch's main concern – the collecting of printed music. This category is to be found among the full scores of operas comprised in volume II of his catalogue, issued in 1930. Because a large number of nineteenth century operas were never engraved and published, or, if engraved, were available for hire only, Hirsch sought to fill some of the gaps with manuscript copies. They include operas by Rossini, Bellini, Konradin Kreutzer, Johann Simon Mayr, Ferdinand Paer, Donizetti, Verdi and Offenbach. This policy also enabled Hirsch to secure the autograph full score of Schreker's opera *Flammen* (c.1898), which is published only in a piano-vocal reduction.

Otherwise, Hirsch had another fifty-odd manuscripts of various types and periods. Excluding plainsong, the earliest is the autograph of Gafori's *Theoriae musicae tractatus* (1480), the same work, with variants, as his *Theoricum opus musice discipline*, printed in that year. An English lute tablature of the late sixteenth century includes music by Antony Holborne and Richard Alison. Besides his splendid collection of the printed 'Airs' of Nicola Matteis, Hirsch had a manuscript volume with an engraved title-page, *Arie diverse per il violino* (c.1690), of which the contents differ from that of any of the printed collections. From the late eighteenth century dates an early and unusual thematic list, *Catalogue de la musique de Monsieur le Conte Ogny*. The autographs of Ernest Toch's *Burlesken*, op.31 (1923), and Holst's carol *Lullay my liking* (1916), round off the miscellanea of the twentieth century.

The manuscripts in the library of the Madrigal Society are an extensive collection of part-books of madrigals and part-songs, the bulk of it having been built up for use in performance at the meetings which the society had regularly from its foundation in 1741. The last of these books dates from about the mid-nineteenth century. One important group, presumably added to the library as a member's gift, comprises a much earlier set, in twenty-three volumes, of part-songs written between the late sixteenth and early seventeenth centuries. (They are discussed in an article by Philip Brett, 'Edward Paston (1550-1630): a Norfolk gentleman and his musical collection', *Transactions of the Cambridge Bibliographical Society*, IV, 1964, 51-69.)

While the manuscripts in the Royal Music Library range from the later part of the sixteenth century, the period of its growth ends, in terms of musical importance, not long after the age of Handel. The earliest item is an autograph volume of 300 canons in the hand of Elway Bevan, dating from about 1611. Almost contemporary is the commonplace book of John Baldwin, a 'singing man of Windsor', who was admitted a Gentleman of the Chapel Royal in 1594 and died in 1615. This is an anthology written out between 1581 and 1606, containing music which he liked from his own time and from the earlier part of the sixteenth century. The royal collection includes two important sources of English virginal music, the compilations made by Benjamin Cosyn (c.1600) and William Forster (1624). Another notable manuscript dating from about the same time contains twenty-three fantasias, some for organ and virginal, others for violins, bass and organ, in the hand of John Coprario, a musician at the court of Charles I, whose arms are on the binding. A folio volume of 245 leaves, dating from about 1690, comprises Henry Purcell's fair copies of a considerable number of his own compositions. (A complementary volume, Add. MS 30930, is in the Department of Manuscripts: see below, p.71.)

The largest group of manuscripts by a major foreign composer consists of operas and chamber duets by Agostino Steffani. There are a dozen operas in his hand. Their presence is probably due to the fact that Steffani was composer at the court of Hanover, whence Georg Ludwig, the Elector, came to succeed to the English throne as George I: he may have brought the manuscripts with him. The most important group of the manuscripts of any one composer in the Royal Music Library comprises the ninety-seven volumes of Handel's autographs, the largest collection of the works of a great composer in any one library. It includes *Messiah* and all Handel's other oratorios, his operas, and most of the major compositions in other categories. (For some other Handel autographs, see below, p.72.) There are also numerous volumes of his music in contemporary manuscript copies. One other autograph from the early eighteenth century deserves mention – twelve concertos, in score, for various instruments, by Alessandro Scarlatti, who began writing them in June 1715. These are among his few instrumental works. The autographs of John Christian Bach (music master to Queen Charlotte) include an opera, *Artaserse*, two Te Deums in D, three Magnificats in C, and a Birthday Ode *Happy morn, auspicious rise.*

Manuscripts in the general collections

The Music Library includes a good deal of manuscript music in the general collections, partly as separate groups or single volumes among a printed collection, partly bound integrally into printed volumes as supplementary matter which is generally contemporary with the edition. These manuscripts are listed in the preliminaries to each of the volumes of the Hughes-Hughes catalogue, when they stand at the end of the index of manuscript numbers, and in pp.86-98 of the Willetts supplement. The following selection may give some idea of the variety.

The earliest manuscript is the altus part of some English songs bound up with the famous *xx Songes* of 1530 (K.1.e.1). The 1580 edition of Lassus's *Sex vocum cantiones* (K.1.c.23) has seven additional motets: all are here anonymous, and only two are found in the corpus of Lassus's music. Byrd's *Psalms, Sonets and Songs* (1588) has a four-part addition 'What pleasures have great princes', apparently his composition. The copy of the 1504 edition of Wollick's *Opus aureum* contains a manuscript complement of four-part settings of Latin texts to Greek metres.

Some pieces in the hand of Albertus Weal have been

added to the unique copy of M. Galilei's *Primo libro d'intavolatura di liuto* (1620). In Benigné de Bacilly's *Airs spirituels* (1672,77) there are manuscript corrections and nine leaves of additional songs, perhaps in his hand. Bound up with some English chamber works of the early eighteenth century (K.7.c.2) are some instrumental airs headed 'Mr. Jenkins his 3 parts for 2 trebels and one bass', c.1680. Purcell's *Choice collection of Lessons for the Harpsichord* (1696) has two extra pieces which, though superscribed with his name, are of doubtful authenticity.

The extensive collection of the printed music of the Noblemen and Gentlemen's Catch Club includes many MS compositions, besides handwritten indexes to the whole, laws and regulations, minutes, records of attendance, etc. The bulky volumes of the Wandering Minstrels contain two interesting autographs – a sketch leaf of Mozart's bearing a draft of the opening theme of the finale of the piano quartet in E flat and some canonic studies K508a, and a 28-bar textless duet composed 1852 for soprano and tenor by Auber. Bound up with the Paris editions of Mozart's sonatas op.1 and op.2, 1763, is the manuscript of a so-called motet, *God is our Refuge*, K20, headed 'by Mr Wolfgang Mozart'. This manuscript which, together with the sonatas, was given to the British Museum in June 1765 by Leopold Mozart, is in fact partly in his hand, and partly in his son's. A volume of French chamber music of the 1740s (K.7.f.16) is unusual in having, bound at both its beginning and end, songs of nearly 100 years later. From the end of the nineteenth century date various manuscripts by Giulio Cottrau – songs, marches and piano pieces, some in his autograph – bound up with two volumes of his printed works, G.691.b, and G.691.c.

Literature

(excluding articles on Hirsch and Royal Music)

King, A. H., 'An English Broadside of the 1520s [the fragmentary song-sheet 'Away mornynge' printed by John Rastell]', *Essays on Opera and English Music, in honour of Sir Jack Westrup*. Edited by F. W. Sternfeld, Nigel Fortune, Edward Olleson. Blackwell: Oxford, 1975, 19-25.

King, A. H., 'The first illustrated and dated Edition of the Marseillaise', *British Museum Quarterly*, XV, 1955, 1-2.

King, A. H., 'The 500th Anniversary of Music Printing. The gradual of c.1473 [I.B. 15154]', *Musical Times*, 114, 1973, 1220-23.

King, A. H., 'Fragments of early printed Music in the Bagford Collection [in Harley 5936]', *Music & Letters*, XI, 1959, 269-73.

King, A. H., 'Lili Marleen', *British Museum Quarterly*, XVII, 1952, 41-2.

King, A.H., 'The Organ Tablature of Johann Woltz', *British Museum Quarterly*, XXV, 1962, 61-3.

King, A. H., 'Rastell reunited'. [On John Rastell's *Interlude* c.1525, the earliest of the Garrick plays, and the *Statutes*, printed by him in 1519, which were originally bound together, became separated, and are both now in the British Library.] *Essays in Honour of Victor Scholderer.* Edited by Dennis E. Rhodes. Pressler: Mainz, 1970, 213-18.

King, A. H., 'The Significance of John Rastell in early Music Printing [on the chronology of the *Interlude* and the broadside printed by him]', *The Library*, Sept. 1971, 197-214.

King, A. H., 'An unrecorded Song ['L'abandonnée'] by Verdi', *British Museum Quarterly*, XXV, 1961, 1-2.

King, A. H., 'Vignettes in early nineteenth-century London Editions of Mozart's Operas', *British Library Journal*, 6, 1980, 24-43.

King, A. H., and Neighbour, O. W., 'Printed Music from the Library of Alfred Cortot', *British Museum Quarterly*, XXXI, 1966-67, 8-16.

Neighbour, O. W., 'Early Editions of John Field', *British Museum Quarterly*, XIX, 1954, 1-2.

Nixon, Howard M., 'The Book of XX Songs [proving that it was not printed by Wynkyn de Worde]', *British Museum Quarterly*, XVI, 1951, 33-5.

Poulton, Diana, and Mitchell, David, 'A list of printed Lute Music in the British Museum', *Lute Society Journal*, 13, 1971, 40-9: 14, 1972, 42-50.

Smith, William C., 'First Editions of Beethoven, Mozart and Haydn,' *British Museum Quarterly*, XI, 1937, 91-2.

Smith, William C., 'First Editions of Schubert', *British Museum Quarterly*, XII, 1938, 24.

Tyson, Alan, *The authentic English Editions of Beethoven*, pp.152. Faber: London, 1963. [Referring to copies in the British Museum, the Bodleian, and the Royal College of Music.]

DEPARTMENT OF PRINTED BOOKS
General Library

This section deals with musical literature in the widest sense. The works named under 'Miscellaneous catalogues and indexes' provide ways of tracing the books about music, of all periods and languages, which are to be found in different areas of the collections.

The other groups in this section include material drawn partly from the General Library and partly from the Music Library, combined in one instance with an index from the Department of Prints and Drawings in the British Museum. Several of the resultant indexes are held in the Music Library for the sake of convenience.

VARIOUS SOURCES

Miscellaneous catalogues and indexes

There is no single, published, cumulated catalogue of the printed musical literature in the Reference Division of the British Library. All books and periodicals relating to music are entered under the appropriate headings in the *General Catalogue of Printed Books.* There are, in addition, some special catalogues devoted to musical literature and various bibliographies through which it can be traced.

Books about music issued from 1880 onwards in all languages are entered in the 'Subject Index', under the heading MUSIC, from which there are some references to cognate headings. Musical material is also found under BALLADS AND SONGS. The first volume was published in 1886 under the title:

> *A Subject Index of modern Works added to the Library of the British Museum in the years 1880-1885.* Compiled by G. K. Fortescue.

Similar volumes, by various hands, each covering five years and including all modern acquisitions from 1886 onwards have been issued at regular intervals. The most recent Index appeared in 1965,66, comprising the years 1956-1960. The series will ultimately be continued in this form to include books published up to the end of 1975. Current musical literature received by copyright is included in *The British Catalogue of Music*, published annually by the British National Bibliography from 1957 to 1973, and since 1974 by the Bibliographical Services Division of the British Library. For earlier books there is:

A manuscript slip-catalogue of musical literature printed before c.1880. Compiled by C. B. Oldman c.1935. (c.2000).

This is well classified and comprises, besides books from the main music section of the library (pressmark 7895, etc.), those in the foundation collections and those acquired in the earlier part of the nineteenth century, all now placed in smaller groups at other pressmarks. This slip-catalogue also includes entries for a number of volumes destroyed by bombing in 1941, some of which, not having been subsequently replaced, have been deleted from the *General Catalogue*. This slip-catalogue may be consulted in the Music Library.

The extensive collection of musical literature in the Hirsch Music Library (see pp.6-8) was catalogued by departmental staff for incorporation into the third edition of the *General Catalogue of Printed Books:*

Catalogue of Printed Books in the British Museum. Accessions. Third series – Part 291B. Books in the Hirsch Library. With supplementary list of music. pp.536. 1959.

Besides entries for all the early works of musical theory, history and bibliography from Bd.1 and Bd.4 of Hirsch's own catalogues, this alphabetical list included some 6000 books of the nineteenth and twentieth centuries that Hirsch had acquired over many years, but had entered only on his own cards. The entries from this Accessions part were incorporated into the third edition of the *General Catalogue of Printed Books.*

Pre-1880 musical literature is also covered within a series of books compiled by R. A. Peddie, and all issued by Grafton, London.

Subject Index of Books published before 1880. A-Z. 1933.

Subject Index of Books published up to and including 1880. Second series A-Z. 1935.
Subject Index of Books published up to and including 1880. Third series. 1939.
Subject Index of Books published up to and including 1880. New series A-Z. 1948.

None of the contents of any of the last three volumes duplicates that of its predecessor. All are based on the holdings of the British Museum, including, however, some titles from other sources. No pressmarks are given, and the entries are very brief. MUSIC and cognate headings supply many useful titles, arranged in chronological order.

For general purposes, there is:

A World Bibliography of Bibliographies. By Theodore Besterman. Second edition. Privately published, 1950.

The heading MUSIC is extensive and most valuable. The majority of the books listed will be found in the British Library.

Exhibition catalogues

No exhibition devoted partly or wholly to music seems to have been held in the British Museum until the later nineteenth century. The first of which a catalogue was issued was:

Guide to the Manuscripts and printed Books illustrating the Progress of musical Notation, exhibited in the Department of Manuscripts and the King's Library. [Edited by (Sir) Edward Maunde Thompson.] pp.20. 1885.

This had no successor until 1901, when there was published:

Guide to the Exhibition in the King's Library illustrating the History of Printing, Music-printing and Bookbinding, pp.vii.163 (last reprinted 1939).

After the Second World War the nature of this exhibition was radically altered, and the comprehensive display of printing was discontinued. There is, however, normally on show in the King's Library a selection of early printed music, illustrative of the main processes, and two more cases of similar books are at the foot of the north-east staircase. At the south end of the King's Library, in the Manuscript Saloon, are several cases of autographs of important musical compositions.

From time to time, since 1949, special exhibitions of music have been mounted. The accompanying publications are as follows:

1 *British Museum. Handel's Messiah. Catalogue of an exhibition held May-July 1951. Arranged in conjunction with the London Choral Society, with the support of the Arts Council of Great Britain.* [By A. H. King.] pp.16. 1951.

The exhibition was held to mark a performance of *Messiah*, given by the London Choral Society in a version by John Tobin and conducted by him.

2 *British Museum. Catalogue of an Exhibition of Music held in the King's Library. October, 1953.* pp.52. [1953.] Mimeographed.

One of a series of exhibitions mounted monthly throughout 1953 to mark the 200th anniversary of the founding of the Museum. The exhibition contained both manuscript and printed music.

3 *Mozart in the British Museum.* [An illustrated catalogue, originally issued for the bicentenary exhibition of 1956. With a general account of the Mozart material in the collections. By A. H. King.] pp.30. 1956. Last reprinted in 1975, by British Museum Publications for the British Library Board.

4 *British Museum. Henry Purcell, 1659(?)-1695. George Frideric Handel, 1685-1759. Catalogue of a commemorative exhibition. May-August 1959.* [By various hands.] pp.47. 8 plates. 1959.

5 *Beethoven. 1770-1827. Catalogue of an exhibition held in the King's Library 28 November 1970 to 28 February 1971.* [By A. H. King.] 1970.

6 *Beethoven and England. An account of sources in the British Museum.* By Pamela J. Willetts. pp.xi.76.pl.xvi. 1970.

Published by the Trustees in connection with the bicentenary exhibition. Includes two appendixes: 1 Music manuscripts of Beethoven in the British Museum. 2 Letters, documents and miscellanea.

7 *Ralph Vaughan Williams. 1872-1958. A guide to the centenary exhibition in the British Museum.* By Pamela J. Willetts. 29 September to 15 December 1972. 1972.

The above publications record a considerable variety of material assembled from several departments of the Museum, sometimes including also items from other British collections, public and private.

Material relating to the history of performance

Libretti

There is no complete catalogue of the libretti of operas, oratorios, cantatas, etc., nor are they placed as an entity. But there is available in the Music Library:

A manuscript slip catalogue, compiled by William Barclay Squire from 1909 to 1914, of libretti in the Department of Printed Books. The slips are arranged under the full title of the work. (c.10,000.)

There are card indexes, which were completed by 1917 and were largely written by Cecilia Stainer, referring from the names of composers and authors to the titles slip.

A small part of the collection has been published in:

Early Dutch Librettos and Plays with Music in the British Museum. By Alfred Loewenberg. pp.30. Aslib: London, 1947.

A substantial acquisition, of 1960, is:

A collection of libretti of operas, operettas, cantatas, with press-cuttings, photographs and other material, dating from c.1820 to 1940, made by Richard Northcott. Pressmark: Northcott.

The Hirsch Music Library contains a small collection of libretti, which are fully listed in vol.IV of Hirsch's catalogue. These, and all other libretti which are catalogued separately, are entered in the *General Catalogue of Printed Books* under the name of the author of the text, or, if he is not named, under the appropriate anonymous heading.

Opera houses

The four following little-known collections are of particular interest for the history of the London opera houses:

1 A collection of cuttings from newspapers, etc., relating to Covent Garden theatre from 1760 to 1843. 2 vol. Th.Cts. 38,39.

2 A collection of newspaper cuttings, etc., relating to Drury Lane Theatre from 1777 to 1834. Th.Cts.40.

3 A collection of cuttings from newspapers relating to the King's and Haymarket Theatres, 1757-1829. 3vol. Th.Cts. 41-43.

4 A collection of cuttings from newspapers, playbills, letters, and other manuscripts relating to the Lyceum Theatre from 1781 to 1840. 3vol. Th.Cts.44-46.

Programmes, etc.

The British Library has a substantial quantity of word-books, programmes, playbills, etc. They have not, however, been kept together as a whole, and their cataloguing is anomalous. The only published list is:

> *British Museum. Register of playbills, programmes and theatre cuttings.* pp.54. [London, c.1950.] Reproduced from typewriting. A copy is in the Music Library, and another at X.985/531. Both have addenda in the hand of C. B. Oldman, recording other playbills (found mostly in the Francis Cox collection of *Fragmenta*, 937.g.17) of early nineteenth century London operas.

The playbills and programmes are mostly in single-sheet folio form, and the collection ranges from the later eighteenth century to c.1940. This *Register* is arranged under towns, and theatres. There are entries for opera houses, music-halls, etc., in both London and the provinces, and for some London pleasure gardens.

A certain number of programmes printed not as single sheets but as booklets, are entered in the *General Catalogue of Printed Books* under the various headings appropriate to the place or institution where the performance took place, or under the responsible authority, eg BBC. A more convenient and more comprehensive treatment is found in the *Catalogue of Printed Music* under the heading PROGRAMMES, in which those in the above *Register* are not entered. Here, miscellaneous collections, relating to concerts given in more than one place, stand first. All other programmes, whether of single concerts or of a series, follow in alphabetical order of the place, to which is added as a subheading, where required, the name of the theatre, hall, or the body responsible for the concert. This collection is predominantly English, but there is a sprinkling of programmes of concerts given in European and other foreign cities. It is kept partly in the Music Library and partly in the General Library.

Perhaps the most notable British collection consists of the programmes amassed by Sir George Smart (Pressmark: Case 61.g and Case 61.h.1-4). It spans the years from 1810 to 1857, and represents private and public concerts, oratorios, and some operas given both in London, and in other cities all over the country, such as Bath, Bristol, Bury St. Edmunds, Cambridge, Derby, Dublin, Edinburgh, Kingston upon Hull, Liverpool, Norwich and Reading. Many of the programmes show that Smart was the conductor. For the main London concert halls such as St. James's Hall, Exeter Hall, and Queen's Hall, there are either fairly long runs of concerts given as a series or a good many single concerts. Concert-giving organizations such as the Sacred Harmonic Society and the (Royal) Philharmonic Society are well covered.

A remarkable collection, consisting almost entirely of London programmes (7892.w.1) seems to have been initiated by Barclay Squire. It amounts to some 8,000 in all. The earliest programmes are in two substantial batches, one from 1847 and another from the 1860s. (These may have been collected by Squire's mother, an amateur singer.) From the 1870s onwards, there is a steady annual accumulation, some of it undoubtedly formed in the years when Squire acted as music critic to a number of papers. (Many programmes have pencil notes in his hand.) The collection finishes in the autumn of 1925, some fifteen months before Squire's death. The concerts took place all over London, in town halls, concert rooms such as Prince's Hall, Piccadilly, Collard's Concert Rooms, Steinway Hall, and at private gatherings such as those held in Edward Dannreuther's house in Orme Square, at the Meistersingers' Club in St. James's Street, and many other similar rendezvous. Those programmes of concerts not heard by Squire himself may have been given to him by his acquaintances among the critics, who included J. A. Fuller Maitland, his brother-in-law.

Some of the programmes of a single occasion have become of historic interest, for instance that of the Richard

Strauss festival held at St. James's Hall in June 1903, at which his wife 'Frau Strauss de Ahna' gave a song recital. Among foreign rarities may be mentioned programmes heard at Rejkavik between 1886 and 1890. A remarkable set of original programmes, chiefly German but also including some French and English, was published by Breitkopf & Härtel, under the title *Konzert* (later *Concert)-Programm-Austausch* from about 1899 onwards. The library has a slightly imperfect set, which is bound in sixty-five folio volumes and runs from vol.2, season 1900, to season 1914 (Pressmark: P.P.1946.ad.). There is one extensive collection recording the work of two distinguished artists, the violinists Adele Fachiri and her sister Jelly d'Arányi. The period covered by the programmes of their concerts begins in 1906 and ends in 1956, and the concerts took place in Britain, Europe and the United States (Pressmark: Arányi).

One notable collection of some 3,000 programmes made by an individual is found at the pressmark 'Henschel'. It covers nearly three-quarters of a century of concert-going by Ernest Henschel, from 1892 to 1938 in Germany (especially in Berlin) and from 1938 to 1966 in England. Much of the latter group comes from smaller halls at which new or unfamiliar works were given. As an example of programmes assembled by a conductor there is a small collection (Pressmark: X.435/115) made by Sir Henry Wood. It begins with a Royal Command concert which he gave at Windsor Castle in 1898, and ends with the programmes, many annotated by him, of some of his last Promenade Concerts at the Royal Albert Hall in 1944. A group of some forty English programmes, and word-books, dating from the late eighteenth century to the late nineteenth, is in the Royal Music Library and derives mostly from occasions patronized by royalty. The programmes can be found under that heading in vol.3. of the *Catalogue of the King's Music Library*, pp.375-9.

Printed programmes held in the Department of Manuscripts are listed on pp.108-9.

London pleasure gardens, etc.

The following little-known collections supplement the standard books on this subject.

1 A collection of newspaper cuttings, advertisements, songs, views, etc. relating to Marylebone Gardens. 1750-c.1850. 840.m.29.

2 A collection of tickets, pamphlets, MS notes, engraved views and portraits, music, and extracts and cuttings from books and periodicals relating to Ranelagh Gardens, made by Jacob Henry Burn. 1743-1841. Cup.401.k.8.

3 A collection relating to Sadler's Wells Theatre, formed by Richard Percival, comprising pamphlets, broadsides, series of playbills and advertisements, songs with music, engraved views and portraits, with autograph letters from actors and others. 14.vol. 1683-1848. Crach.1Tab.b.4.

4 A collection of tickets, bills of performances, pamphlets, MS notes, engravings, and extracts and cuttings from books and periodicals relating to Vauxhall Gardens, made by Jacob Henry Burn. 1709-1874. Cup.401.k.7.

5 A collection of cuttings from newspapers, advertisements, playbills, etc., compiled by I. Fillinham. Vol.5 includes prints, pamphlets, cuttings, etc. relating to the Fireworks in Green Park, a display which was held on 27 April 1749, to mark the Peace of Aix-La-Chapelle, and for which Handel wrote the music. 1889.b.10/5.

Iconography

The four following card indexes are available in the Music Library:

1 Portraits of musicians, including a selection of those in the Department of Prints and Drawings in the British Museum.

The latter consist entirely of engraved portraits, for which the cards have been copied from the index compiled by Arthur Mayger Hind, Keeper of Prints and Drawings, 1933-45. The portraits recorded from the Music Library consist largely of frontispieces to musical publications or illustrations on their title pages. The cards (c.2100) provide short descriptions, giving either references to the catalogues of the Department of Prints and Drawings, or the pressmarks of the Music Library. Musical portraits of various kinds held in the Department of Manuscripts are listed on pp.92-100.

2 Operatic scenes, mostly on title-pages of music in the Music Library. Arranged under the name of the composer. (80)

3 Illustrations of performers, found in British and foreign printed music and works of musical theory.

Arranged in four groups – a single performer, two, three, and four or more performers. The illustrations of a single performer are arranged according to the name of the instrument. The second and third groups are arranged according to the name of the salient instrument. The last group is arranged chronologically, and ranges from 1480 to c.1860. (c.600)

4 Illustrations of instruments, without players, found in British and foreign printed music and works of musical theory.

Arranged in four groups – a single instrument, two, three, and four or more instruments. The first three groups are arranged under the name of the instrument or salient instrument. The last group is arranged chronologically, and ranges from 1532 to 1916. (c.350)

Collecting and dispersal of music

A primary source of information is:

List of Catalogues of English Book Sales 1676-1900 now in the British Museum. [By Harold Mattingly, I. A. K. Burnett, A. W. Pollard.] pp.xv.523. 1915.

Contains numerous catalogues of music libraries formed by private collectors. An interleaved copy of the *List* was maintained by A. N. L. Munby (d.1974) who had entered in it by hand a vast number of additional sale catalogues, including many of music, found in other libraries. A bound xerox of his copy is in the North Library. All named collections were excerpted and printed in A. Hyatt King's *Some British Collectors of Music*, Cambridge University Press: Cambridge, 1963, which also includes important London auctions from 1915 onwards. The *List* also comprises catalogues of the sales of anonymous collections and of music publishers' stocks, plates, etc. These are not in *Some British Collectors*, but are included in a fairly complete typescript of all the musical items in the *List*, made by Donald Wakeling and O. E. Deutsch, c.1940. A copy of this typescript is in the Music Library, where there are also three card catalogues germane to this subject:

1 A select index of printed music sold at auction, principally in London by Sotheby's, and by antiquarian music dealers, from 1877 to c.1965. The dealers' catalogues analysed are those issued by the First Edition Bookshop, Otto Haas, and Kenneth Mummery. Each card gives the composer's name, short title, place of imprint and date, price and reference. (c.8,500)

2 A select index of manuscript music sold at auction, principally in London, by Sotheby's and by antiquarian music dealers, from 1877 to c.1965. The dealers' catalogues analysed are those issued by the First Edition Bookshop, Otto Haas and Kenneth Mummery. Each card gives the composer's name, the title, approximate date, price and reference. (c.1,200)

3 A list of dedications and signatures written on the title-pages, fly-leaves, etc. of printed music in the Music Library by British and foreign musicians from the late eighteenth century onwards. The cards, arranged under the names of the writers, bear the title of the work, its date and pressmark. (c.750)

As a parergon to the *List of Catalogues of English Book Sales* (1 above), there may be mentioned:

Music in English Auction Sales, 1676-1750. A dissertation presented for the degree of Doctor of Philosophy at the University of London by Lenore F. Coral. 1974. (Copy in London University Library.)

This examines the catalogues of 458 book sales which included music, musical theory and musical literature and provides analytical indexes of owners and titles. While the majority of the catalogues are in the British Library, this dissertation also records others from a variety of British and foreign libraries, partly derived from the research of Dr. Coral herself and partly from the work of A. N. L. Munby.

Music printing and publishing

The four following card catalogues are available in the Music Library:

1 *Topographical music printing* A catalogue of all music in the Music Library, printed before 1801, but excluding British imprints, giving short title, date and pressmark and arranged under country, town, and name of printer. (c.8,500)

2 *Publishers' catalogues* A catalogue of the catalogues, now in the Music Library and in the General Library, issued by British and foreign music publishers from the early 18th century up to c.1870. Some of the catalogues were issued as separate publications, but most were printed by way of advertisement as an integral part of a piece of music. The cards are arranged alphabetically under the publishers' names. (c.1,300)

3 *Subscribers' lists* A catalogue of lists of subscribers to musical publications, now in the Music Library, predominantly British, but including also a few foreign lists. The cards, which are arranged in chronological order, range from 1711 to c.1890. (c.670)

4 *London publishers, etc.* An index of music publishers, sellers, printers and engravers working in London from 1850 to 1950. Besides name, address and activity, each card gives dates of occupancy of premises. These data are derived from the classified section of the Post Office Directories. (c.2,500) Information about London publishers active during the period before 1850 is included in Charles Humphries and William C. Smith's *Music Publishing in the British Isles*, 2nd edition, Blackwell: Oxford, 1970.

Literature

Tilmouth, Michael, 'A Calendar of References to Music in Newspapers published in London and the Provinces (1660-1719) [principally the Burney Collection in the Department of Printed Books in the British Library]', *Royal Musical Association Research Chronicle*, I, 1961, ii-vii, 1-107.

Coral, Lenore, 'A John Playford Advertisement [Harley

5936/421, in the Bagford Collection]', *Royal Musical Association Research Chronicle*, 5, 1967, 1-12.

Instrument makers

The following card catalogue is available in the Music Library:
London musical instrument makers, 1840-1950.
A catalogue of names and addresses, with dates of occupancy of premises, based on the classified section of the Post Office Directories. It is divided into four sections: 1 Musical boxes. 2 Unspecified instruments. 3 Specified instruments other than pianoforte. 4 Pianoforte. (4874)

THE SCOPE OF THE COLLECTIONS

The collections of printed musical literature are comprehensive for most periods and languages, and are generally complementary to the range of the printed music. Since the majority of books, at any rate the more recent ones, are by no means uncommon, it is hardly necessary, even if it were practicable, to give a detailed account of them. This section will therefore record some of the early, rare or unusual items, or groups of items, in a number of selected categories. English books will be mentioned only when they are little known or of some special interest.

Dictionaries

The tally of dictionaries opens with one of the eight recorded copies of Tinctoris's *Terminorum musicae diffinitorium* (Treviso, c.1494), and includes most of those listed in the various classes under the heading 'Dictionaries' in *The New Grove*. There are a few interesting special copies, such as the one of J. G. Walther's *Musicalisches Lexicon* (1732) with six pages of interesting additions in a nearly contemporary hand.

History

The collections are well provided with books which date from the beginnings of musical historiography, including all important general works from the time of Martini onwards. Among several copies of Sir John Hawkins's *General History of the Science and Practice of Music* (1776), there are two of special interest. One was owned by the author himself, and has many notes in his hand: the other belonged to Burney, whose marginal comments are illuminating and sometimes sardonic.

Biography

One of the most numerous categories in the library relates to the biography of musicians of every kind, whether it be their own memoirs or critical studies by others. There is also a wealth of diaries and memoirs of all periods containing musical observation and comment. Perhaps the earliest example of collective biography is Mattheson's *Grundlage einer Ehren-Pforte* (1740), which describes the lives of 149 musicians, past and present. It precedes by nearly a generation the first biography of a single composer, John Mainwaring's *Memoirs of the Life of the late George Frederic Handel* (1760), of which the copy owned by George III was unfortunately destroyed in the war. (It has been replaced by another copy in contemporary binding.) Perhaps the largest quantity of books about any one composer, or a school, is that which reflects the enduring attraction of the Viennese classics, especially Beethoven and Mozart. For the latter the collections are remarkably comprehensive, thanks notably to the assemblage in the Hirsch Library. It is perhaps worth mentioning one book which was lacking even there, and had never been received by copyright deposit. This was Alberto B. Bach's *Mozart, Raphael and the Renaissance* (Edinburgh, 1890), so elusive that after years of search it was purchased from abroad. As an adjunct to biography, the published writings of a composer are important, as witness the large collection of Wagner's literary and critical works, in the original and translation, in first and early editions. One characteristic of the biographical collections is due to the attention paid to the principle of acquiring as many books as possible written about a composer in his native language and published in his country, eg works about Liszt issued in Hungary.

Theory

The library received its first substantial accession of early works of musical theory – the term is used here in its most comprehensive sense – in 1778 when the Trustees accepted two gifts of books from Sir John Hawkins, on 30 May and 23 October, about fifty volumes in all, chiefly Italian. Among the most notable were two by Gafori, *Practica musicae* (1502), and *Divinum opus musicae* (1508). The sustained acquisition of such literature has amassed, besides most of the other books written by Gafori (many decorated with fine woodcuts), the classic works of Pietro Aaron, Vincenzo Galilei, Giovanni Spataro, and Zarlino. An example of Aaron's work, in his manuscript, is found in the only recorded copy of the 1507 edition of the *Regula musice plane* by Bonaventura de Brixia. Bound up with it are ten leaves headed 'Delli principij de tuti li toni secondo mi Pietro Aron', which may be the original draft of his *Trattato della natura et cognitione di tutti gli tuoni de canto figurato.* Two of the earliest Italian books in this field are Burtius's *Musices opusculum* (1487) and Francesco Caza's *Tractato vulgare de canto figurato* (1492), a unique copy.

The equally important field of early German theory is fully represented by such books as the *Dodekachordon* of Heinrich Glareanus (1547), Hugo Spechshart, *Flores musice omnis cātus gregoriani* (1488), Johann Frosch, *Rerum musicalium opusculum* (1535), and Martin Agricola, *Musica instrumentalis Deudsch* (1529), most of his other treatises, printed at Wittenberg by his friend Georg Rhaw. Many of these rarities are found in the Hirsch Library, in fine copies. The collections are very strong in the voluminous works of the eighteenth century German theorists – Mattheson (a score of them), Adlung, Marpurg and Kirnberger, as also of their French counterparts such as Rameau. Thanks, again, in part to the Hirsch collection, this coverage extends right on to the outstanding theorists of the nineteenth and twentieth century, from the works of Catel, Reicha, Cherubini and Dehn to the treatises of Schenker, Schoenberg and Schillinger.

Opera

Among the extensive range of books on opera there is a copy of Leone Allacci's *Drammaturgia* (1666), a scarce volume, and one of the earliest reference works in this field. Another noteworthy Italian book is a copy of Count Algarotti's *Saggio sopra l'opera in musica* (1763), which the Trustees received from the author on 27 May of that year, by the hand of Thomas Hollis, the 'republican'. (This was the first printed book on music given to the Museum from abroad.) A scarce French work is the first, 1754, edition of the *Dictionnaire portatif des théâtres . . . de Paris*, by Antoine de Leris, of which the eighty-five word title includes an indication of its considerable value for information about singers, librettists, composers and much else relating to opera.

Instruments

The extensive collections include a copy of the earliest general book in the subject, Sebastian Virdung's *Musica getutscht* (1511), with its many vivid woodcuts. It is complemented, just over a century later, by Praetorius's *Theatrum instrumentorum* (1625), (which forms part of his great *Syntagma musicum*) and, among French writers, by Mersenne's *Harmonicorum instrumentorum libri iv* (1636). The library's copies of both these books are very fine. For books on a particular instrument, those on the organ are probably the most numerous. Here again, the earliest book of note is a German one – Arnolt Schlick's *Spiegel der Orgelmacher* (1512), of which the library has one of the two known copies. This is in the Hirsch collection, which also has a superb copy of the most handsome and important books on this instrument – the three-volume work by François Bédos de Celles, *L'art du facteur d'orgues* (1766-78), which is matched by the German contemporary, Jacob Adlung's *Musica mechanica organoedi* (1768), a primary source of information about organs in Germany.

In the wealth of books about pianos, one special collection deserves mention – the material amassed by James Leslie Stephen, partly printed, partly manuscript, relating to the construction and history of the instrument (including player-pianos), English and European. It ranges from the mid-1870s to about 1950, and is grouped into thirteen categories, such as specifications, fittings and frames, actions, drawings of cases, manufacturers' catalogues, exhibition catalogues, and the like (Pressmark: 07902.b.1/1-13). Among books on the violin, two deserve special mention – a sumptuous copy of L. A. Vidal's three-volume work *Les Instruments à archet* (1876-78) and one of the limited, large paper edition of the rare French translation of W. H. Hill's classic, *Antoine Stradivarius* (1908).

Some of the most attractive early illustrations of non-European instruments are found in the notable work of F. B. Solvyns. It was first published in Calcutta, in 1799, as *A Collection of two hundred and fifty coloured Etchings descriptive of the Manners, Customs and Dresses of the Hindoos.* Section XI comprises 36 plates each of which, in large folio, shows a performer with his instrument. A selection appeared in London in 1804, in large quarto, as *The Costume of Hindostan*, but only 11 of the 60 plates show musicians. But when Solvyns' book was produced in Paris, greatly expanded in four almost elephant folio volumes, entitled simply *Les Hindoues*, the second, issued in 1810, contained 70 plates of musicians. (The detailed accompanying text, in French and English, describes the use and nature of the instruments.) The plates show numerous stringed instruments, many kinds of drum and other percussion, trumpets, and a few woodwind. The name of each instrument, in text and caption, is given in a romanization, which can be identified, without much difficulty, with the modern term. All the foregoing editions are found in the General Library. The Department of Prints and Drawings in the British Museum has a set of Solvyns' work (registration number 1835-7-11-97), entitled on the binding 'Etchings of Hindoo Costume'. The plates of instruments in vol.1, nos.94 to 129, correspond to those of the 1799 edition.

As an appendage to books on instruments, there may be mentioned what is perhaps the best known of books on instrumentation – Berlioz's *Grande traité d'instrumentation*, first issued in 1843. Of this the library has a copy which was

Berlioz's own, and has annotations in his hand, as well as the two German translations. The record of these, issued in 1864, was the one made, with the composer's approval, by Alfred Dörffel (who also translated into German Berlioz's *Le chef d'orchestre*).

Periodicals

A generous range of musical journals begins with Marpurg's *Critische Musicus an der Spree* (Berlin, 1749-50), of which the library's copy is the only one recorded by RISM in the United Kingdom. The full historical development of this musico-literary form can be traced in the collections, which include the organs of learned societies devoted to music, annuals on special topics, or particular composers, and the like. The mainstream of these periodicals deals with music in the western, European tradition, enriched, in its later stages, by a swelling tributary of titles that reflect the rapidly expanding study of the music of other continents.

The holding of British periodicals falls into two broad categories. The larger comprises specifically musical journals, of which, from their inception in the 1770s up to about 1860, there were some fifty. These included such enduring ones as *The Musical World* (1838-91) and *The Musical Times* (1844 to date). Concurrently, there appeared another type, characteristic perhaps of the United Kingdom, periodicals devoted to music and other arts: in some of them music was not mentioned on the title-page, and in others it was not given precedence. Many of these journals were short-lived and are now rare, and not perhaps well known, but their musical content is often of significant interest, not least for their reviews. Such, to give but four examples in the library's holding, are *The Parthenon. A magazine of art and literature* (1825-26); *The Sunbeam. A weekly journal devoted to polite literature and music* (1838-39); *The British Minstrel, and musical and literary Miscellany* (1842-45); *The Connoisseur. A journal of music and the fine arts* (1845-46).

Bibliography

The collections have a fair number of those publications which list, with some continuity, the music issued in national or regional bibliographies. The oldest, and probably the most famous, is that known successively by the names of 'Whistling' and 'Hofmeister'. (The very complicated nature of this work cannot be discussed here. Details are given in Rudolf Elvers and Cecil Hopkinson, 'A survey of the music catalogues of Whistling and Hofmeister', *Fontes artis musicae*, XIX, 1972, 1-7. Hofmeister himself provided some historical details in his preface to Theil 3 of the volume that appeared in 1845.) The library's fairly complete set comprises most of the volumes and parts of the *Handbuch der musikalischen Literatur* compiled from 1817 onwards by C. F. Whistling, and the second volume issued for him by Friedrich Hofmeister (covering the years 1829-33 and 1834-38) with the latter's second and third supplements covering 1829-33 and 1834-38. These are followed by the cumulative volumes covering music published 1844-51, 1852-59, 1860-67, 1868-73, and thereafter quinquennially up to 1919-23. The set also includes the annual volumes of Hofmeister's *Verzeichnis der Musikalien* (as his monthly publications were ultimately entitled) for 1853 to 1860, and 1868-1974. The great merit of this long-lived bibliography is that it included not only the alphabetical and classified lists of music, all with prices, issued in 'Germany and the countries bordering it', and, to a lesser extent in France and Italy, but also musical literature, published portraits and other representations of musicians.

The library also has a much less well known English counterpart, which is to be found in *The Musical Directory, Register and Almanack*, issued in London by Rudall, Rose and Carte (later Rudall, Carte), from 1853 to 1931. The volumes from 1853 up to 1907 contain a substantial, broadly classified list of music published in England.

Miscellanea

The Music Library holds the archive of the Wandering Minstrels, an English amateur society, of a strongly aristocratic character, which gave concerts, often for charity, from 1860 to 1898, principally in London and the home counties. This comprehensive collection (K.6.e.1-7) is valuable as a record of a vanished world: it comprises programmes, numerous photographs, letters, accounts, prints and drawings of musical interest, and various other documents, a manuscript catalogue of the library, badges and other mementos. Further details are given by A. H. King, 'The Wandering Minstrels', in Horst Leuchtmann (ed.), *Festschrift für Kurt Dorfmüller*, Munich, 1983.

Literature

King, A. H., 'A Collection of musical Programmes [formed by Ernst Henschel]', *British Museum Quarterly*, XXXIII, 1965, 91-2.

Paisey, David, 'A Collection of German religious Songs of the mid-sixteenth Century', *British Library Journal*, 1, 1975, 71-83.

Paisey, David, 'Some occasional Aspects of Hermann Schein', *British Library Journal*, 1, 1975, 171-80.

Meyer, Kathi, 'The liturgical music Incunabula in the British Museum', *The Library*, ser.4, no.20, 1939, 272-94.

DEPARTMENT OF MANUSCRIPTS

Introductory note

Throughout this section italic type is used to denote the title of a work. This is at variance with the practice of the Department of Manuscripts, in whose catalogues roman type, with single quotation marks, has been preferred for this purpose.

Manuscript numbers are generally given only for fragments or small pieces found in miscellaneous composite volumes, and for certain anthologies and the like. The name of the collection (Harley, Sloane, Cotton, etc.) is given only for those manuscripts dating from the time of the Museum's foundation or from its early years, or for a special group (Egerton, etc.). A manuscript denoted solely by a number, occasionally of four figures, but mostly of five, without any prefix, belongs to the Additional series. For general information about the foundation and special collections, reference should be made to M. A. E. Nickson's *The British Library. Guide to the catalogues and indexes of the Department of Manuscripts*, The British Library: London, 1978.

A notable manuscript, such as Egerton 2615 (see p.66) is included in *The New Grove*, in the article SOURCES, vol.17, pp.639 et seqq. Some fifty other British Library manuscripts of comparable importance are also to be found in this article, which is arranged by categories, and according to period or country. The relevant entries give the British Library number and date of each manuscript, a summary of contents, and mention editions of it, with references to related books and other literature. Many of these important manuscripts are included in this section of the present book.

THE CATALOGUES

Catalogue of the Manuscript Music in the British Museum. [By Thomas Oliphant.] pp.105. 1842.

This was the first attempt to catalogue the manuscript music. (For the circumstances of Oliphant's work, see King, *Printed*

Music in the British Museum, etc. pp.60-62.) It made no attempt at classification and identified the manuscripts by a sequence of numbers independent of those used in the other departmental catalogues. Oliphant's catalogue is now of only historical interest, although it is perhaps worth noting that Eitner's *Quellen-Lexikon* (1900-04) used its numbers for reference.

Catalogue of Manuscript Music in the British Museum. By Augustus Hughes-Hughes.

vol.I Sacred music. pp.xxvi.615. 1906.
vol.II Secular vocal music. pp.xxv.961. 1908.
vol.III Instrumental music, treatises, etc. pp.xx.543. 1909.

All three volumes were reprinted photolithographically in 1964-66. It should perhaps be noted at the outset that this catalogue excludes unharmonized liturgical music. Such manuscripts can however be traced in vols.74, 76 and 77 of the Class Catalogue of MSS which is available in the Students' Room of the Department. Vol.74 comprises Service Books and Commentaries; vol.76, Service Books. Vol.1 Latin; vol.77, Service Books, Vol.II Latin and modern languages. Such manuscripts are also fully described in the published catalogues of the collections or series to which they belong. Eighteen of the most significant are included, with full bibliographical references, in *The New Grove*, in the article SOURCES, vol.17, pp.612-34.

In the Hughes-Hughes catalogue, the manuscripts are listed and described throughout according to musical categories. A manuscript containing only a single musical work is entered in only one category, but one containing a variety of works is entered in as many categories as required. Such manuscripts are described as an entity not in Hughes-Hughes' catalogue but in that of the collection or series to which they belong. (The same is true of manuscripts containing literary or other material together with music.) But in all such cases, the fullest musical detail is found only in Hughes-Hughes. Each volume of the Hughes-Hughes catalogue has two indexes, one of initial words and titles, the other of names and subjects. In vol.III, part V, section VII, there is a useful index of drawings and descriptions of musical instruments both singly and in groups. A predecessor of this index is in:

Early Drawings and Illuminations. An introduction to the study of illustrated manuscripts with a dictionary of subjects in the British Museum. By Walter de Gray Birch and Henry Jenner. pp.xiii.310. Bagster: London, 1879.

The entry 'music' in the 'dictionary' refers to numerous representations of instruments, but the nomenclature is rather out of date by modern standards of iconography.

A useful, select list of instruments depicted in illuminated manuscripts now in the British Library is included in *Old English Instruments of Music* by F. W. Galpin, fourth edition, revised by Thurston Dart (Methuen: London, 1965), pp.222-231, 'Some illustrations of musical instruments in manuscripts, carvings and paintings from the eighth century to the eighteenth century'.

Music acquired by the British Museum after the completion of the Hughes-Hughes catalogue is to be found in:

Handlist of Music Manuscripts acquired 1908-67. Pamela J. Willetts. pp.vii.112. 1970.

This *Handlist*, which has a comprehensive index of names, is divided into two main categories – Additional Manuscripts and Egerton Manuscripts. The sequence of the 'Additional' series is chronological, by years, and within each year the manuscripts are arranged according to 'Additional' numbers. The 'Egerton' series is arranged in numerical order. The other sections of the *Handlist* comprise 'Music manuscripts in the Music Room, Department of Printed Books', and 'Music manuscripts on loan to the Department of Manuscripts'.

The former section, dealing with what is now the 'Music Library', includes manuscripts in the Hirsch Library, miscellaneous manuscripts in the Royal Music not in the published catalogues, and manuscripts bound up with volumes consisting largely of printed music.

The other section of the *Handlist* records the most valuable portion of the library of the Royal Philharmonic Society, of which the first part was deposited in 1914, when there was published:

Catalogue of the musical Manuscripts deposited on loan in the British Museum by the Royal Philharmonic Society of London. pp.16. 1914.

Subsequent deposits made by the society are set out in the *Handlist*, and include a collection of some 6,000 letters (now bound in thirty-eight volumes), manuscript scores of works commissioned by the society, and minute books (directors' meetings and general meetings) which date from its foundation in 1813 onwards. A further deposit of the society's papers was made in 1978, and the remainder of the printed and manuscript music was transferred from the Royal Academy of Music in 1983: details are given under 'Loan 48' in the register of manuscripts on loan that is available in the Students' Room of the Department of Manuscripts.

A rough list of all music manuscripts acquired since the publication of the *Handlist* by P. J. Willetts is available in the Students' Room. It is entitled: *Handlist of Music Manuscripts acquired since 1968.* Like its predecessor, it is divided into three groups – Additional, Egerton and loans.

The department's manuscripts of polyphonic music dating from the eleventh century to the sixteenth century are described, in an international context, in three volumes of the *Repertoire internationale des sources musicales* (*RISM*), as follows, the relevant page references being given after the publication date:

Manuscripts of polyphonic Music. 11th-early 14th century. Edited by Gilbert Reaney. G. Henle: München, 1960. pp.491-522. (*RISM* B IV^1.)

Manuscripts of polyphonic Music. (c.1320-1400.) By Gilbert Reaney. G. Henle: München, 1969. pp.224-241. (*RISM* B IV^2.)

Handschriften mit mehrstimmige Musik des 14., 15. und 16. Jahrhunderts. Beschrieben und inventarisiert von Kurt von Fischer. G. Henle: München, 1972. pp.607-660; pp.675-725 (the Old Hall Manuscript, acquired by the British Library in 1973 – Add. MS 57950). (*RISM* B IV^4.)

In each of these three volumes, the descriptions of the manuscripts are followed by an enumeration of articles about them and of any editions of the music in whole or part.

The department's manuscripts of lute and guitar music are described in another volume of the *Repertoire internationale des sources musicales* (RISM):

Handschriftlich überlieferte Lauten- und Gitarren-

tablaturen des 15. bis 18. Jahrhunderts. Beschriebende Katalog von Wolfgang Boetticher. G. Henle: München, 1978, pp.172-193. (RISM B VII)

Some important material relating to dramatic and vocal music in London during the first part of the nineteenth century is to be found in the collection of the Lord Chamberlain's plays. The catalogue is:

British Museum. Catalogue of Additions to the Manuscripts. Plays submitted to the Lord Chamberlain, 1824-1851. Additional Manuscripts 42865-43038. [Compiled largely by P. D. A. Harvey.] pp.viii.359. 1964.

The manuscripts are arranged according to their numbers, in chronological order. There is an author index and a title index. The 'plays' include a considerable number of opera libretti, which can be traced either by the author or translator of the text, or by the title. Sometimes the manuscript of the 'play' is accompanied by a copy of the printed libretto, some of which are lacking in the Department of Printed Books, but are not entered in its *General Catalogue.* Among foreign operatic composers represented by the manuscript of a libretto adapted for a London production, are Mozart, Weber, Winter, Bellini, Donizetti, Rossini and Verdi. The collection also includes some songs licensed for the stage 1826 to 1833, 'addresses' to famous singers such as Madame Vestris, and some letters by various composers such as Bishop and Balfe.

Handlists of the Lord Chamberlain's play collection, maintained in continuation of the above catalogue, are available in the Students' Room.

THE SCOPE OF THE COLLECTIONS

Music

The richness of these collections lies in their extensive holding of music by British composers, from the middle ages to the present day – a holding whose origins can be traced in the Foundation collections of the British Museum. Like other major libraries in Europe, the museum early determined to assemble a national archive, and so gave priority to British manuscripts of all kinds, including music, and to documents, letters and the like, relating to it. With limited funds, the purchase of manuscripts by foreigners, even the most famous, was necessarily very selective. It is nevertheless remarkable in the case of music how well represented in the collections are the works of some of the greatest European musicians (partly through generous gifts and bequests, and partly through loans), as certain periods in the following summary will show.

One of the earliest pieces of vocal music is a group of Latin texts, in a MS of the tenth century (Royal 15 B.xix, ff.125v,127) notated in neums. From the eleventh century onwards come a group of miracle plays with music, including the famous *Play of Daniel*, written at Beauvais about 1230 (Egerton 2615, ff.95-108). Of about the same date as this play is the unique, very famous six-part round *Sumer is icumen in*, composed c.1250 (Harley 978, f.11v). The same volume includes, on ff.9v,10, the famous motet *Ave mater gloriosa*. Another Harley manuscript (4604,f.182v), includes an early fourteenth century canon *Nunc sancte nobis spiritus*, apparently written for Coldingham Priory, Berwickshire, to which there is an amusing complement in a song *Vulneratur Karitas*, a setting of a poem, of about 1300, which records the 'degeneracy of the age' (Harley 746, f.107).

An important manuscript (28550) dating from c.1325 and comprising largely a Register of Robertsbridge Abbey in Sussex, includes two fragmentary and four complete pieces for organ or clavicembalum (the earliest known in England), two of the latter being original compositions, and two arrangements of Fauvel motets (ff.43-44v). From Fountains Abbey in Yorkshire come some fragments of sequences and hymns of the fourteenth century, and some fragmentary mass settings and motets of the fifteenth (40011B). Similar is the MacVeagh fragment (41667I, ff.26-27v) comprising some motets and a ballad. Another group of fragments contains music by John Plummer and John Dunstable (54324). The collections contain a good many other such pieces from this period, largely of continental origin, to French and Latin texts. These are, of course, but a tiny proportion of the very large quantity of music written in the Middle Ages. Similarly, the survival of substantial volumes is very rare from this period. One is the famous 'Old Hall' manuscript (57950), which contains polyphonic Mass settings and motets written for the Chapel Royal by some thirty composers in the reign of Henry IV, with additions of c.1420. The other is the so-called *Windsor Carol-Book*, which dates from 1430 to 1444 (Egerton 3307): it comprises polyphonic liturgical works, for Holy Week and Easter, 33 carols, and a drinking song, probably composed for St. George's Chapel, Windsor.

From the very early years of the sixteenth century comes a typical collection of Italian Renaissance music – *frottole, strambotti* and odes, with four-part vocal works by such masters as Josquin des Près, F. de Luprano and G. Fogliani (Egerton 3051). Two rather similar collections comprise madrigals, *ballate, caccie*, by lesser known Italian composers (apparently written for a member of the Medici family) (29987, ff.26-69v) and three-part chansons, by mostly anonymous Flemish composers (35087). In England, the Renaissance saw a new flowering of music that began in the reign of Henry VIII. It was for him and Katherine of Aragon that there was written a collection of four-part motets (Royal 8 G.vii), and his name also appears among the composers in a large collection of three-part songs (31922) almost certainly used at his court. The Ritson manuscript (5665) is a similar, slightly earlier, volume of motets, carols, secular duets, etc. A collection of four-part masses by Nicholas Ludford (Royal Appendix 45-48) dates from before 1536, the year when Katherine of Aragon died: the binding bears both her arms and those of Henry VIII. From the last years of Henry's reign dates the famous anthology of organ solos compiled and arranged, with some cithern music, by Thomas Mulliner: this too bears the king's arms (30513). Complementary to this music are such manuscripts as a record of payments to musicians and instrument makers from the Household-book of Henry VIII, apparently in 1525 and 1526 (Egerton 2604) and a list of dance-tunes popular in the early sixteenth century (Sloane 3501, f.2v).

The mid-sixteenth century saw an upsurge of church music, of which a large collection, written about 1547-8, is included in Royal Appendix 74-76. There are anthems, services and hymns (and, in addition, various pieces for stringed instruments). Another extensive repertory of four-part church music is found in some well-known books (17802-17805) which date mostly from within the third quarter of this century, and are known from the name of an early owner Dr. Philip Gyffard, as the 'Gyffard part-books'. Tallis, Blytheman, Sheppard, Taverner and Redford are among the best known composers. (John Redford was both dramatist and composer: a manuscript (15233) dating from about 1550 includes some plays with music and some organ fantasias by him.) Royal Appendix 17-22, 23-25, 26-30, 31-35, 49-54 comprise an extensive collection of Latin motets (with some chansons and madrigals) ranging from four to ten voices, by a Flemish composer named Derike Gerarde, in the service of the Earl of Arundel. Compared with the enormous quantity of English church music, the representation of that for the church of Scotland is sparse. There is a tenor part of a Te Deum composed about 1575-78 by Andrew Kemp of St. Andrews (33933, f.48v), and his name occurs also in the same volume (ff.44v-71v) containing the contra-tenor of half-a-dozen Scottish metrical psalms. Ff.1-48 of this volume have the contra-tenor part of 88 psalms set by David Peables, and of twelve canticles by Kemp and other composers.

From the early years of this century onwards, the collections are increasingly rich in music for viols, in anything from three to eight parts, much of the earlier music being arranged from vocal works of various kinds. One notable manuscript contains over 100 such pieces (31390, ff.25v-65), dating from about 1578, and (rather unusually) entitled *A booke of In nomines and other solfainge songs of v,vi,vii and viii parts for voyces or instruments.* An earlier portion of the same manuscript (ff.2-21v) contains six-part viol music, including one piece 'O salutaris hostia' which bears Byrd's name. (In this connection may be mentioned a document in Byrd's autograph, a certificate written in 1581 on behalf of Dorothy Tempest, Egerton 3722.)

By the seventeenth century the variety of instrumental music begins to increase. From its early years comes part of a manuscript (29996, ff.196v, 204v) containing two works for four hands at one keyboard – 'A verse for two to play on one virginall or organs', by Nicholas Carleton, and a fancy, by

Thomas Tomkins. To the same time belong twelve fancies for organ and two bass viols, by John Coprario (31416), apparently in his autograph. A large volume of seventy pieces for organ by John Bull dates from 1628; they were probably composed while he was organist at Antwerp Cathedral. For the lute, there is the famous collection (Egerton 2046, ff.14-51v) of dances and other tunes arranged by Jane Pickeringe in 1616.

From the time of Charles I dates a collection of Welsh airs for the harp (14905, ff.10-53), by various composers, written in a kind of tablature. Among a large quantity of viol music may be mentioned an anthology (40657-61) for two to six instruments, made at some time before 1645. It includes autograph works by William Lawes, other pieces by a dozen of his contemporaries and some arrangements of madrigals by Marenzio, Monteverdi and other Italian masters. An unusual book of lyra-viol music, with songs, is that compiled by Silvanus Stirrop (56279), which includes some of his own music and pieces by such musicians as Thomas Ford, Tobias Hume and Nicholas Lanier. Another collection of lyra-viol pieces (59869) dates from c.1650 to c.1680, and includes music by Simon Ives, John Jenkins and William Lawes. Keyboard music of the Commonwealth is well represented by the virginal book of Elizabeth Rogers, dated 27 February 1656, seventy-nine pieces, mainly anonymous songs and dances, arranged for the instrument. A work by Matthew Lock, 'for His Majesty's Sagbutts and Cornets', partly in his autograph (17801, ff.62-5), is supposed to have been written to mark the progress of Charles II through London on 22 April 1661.

Foreign instrumental music includes a collection of lute pieces (16899, ff.72-75, 88-111v), dating from about 1615-1618, inserted at the end of the *Album Amicorum* of Frederic de Botnia, of Saumur. There is a group of twenty-two organ pieces (34898, ff.1-16, 23v-31), of about 1628, mostly sacred and probably composed by J. U. Steigleder. A miscellaneous Sloane manuscript (1021), written about 1640 by Johann Stobaeus of Königsberg, Kapellmeister to the Elector of Brandenburg, contains numerous lute pieces. From some forty years later there dates a collection of ninety lute pieces

(Sloane 2923, ff.3v-36, 101v-115) mostly in the hand of 'J. A. K.', possibly J. A. Kämpfer, and supposedly a kinsman of Engelbert Kämpfer, the famous German traveller in the Near and Far East, in whose writing the rest of the manuscript is.

Among a wealth of English vocal music, one remarkable collection (29372-29377), made by Thomas Myriell, has an engraved title-page which reads thus: *Tristitiae remedium. Cantiones selectissimae diversorum tum authorum tum argumentorum labore et manu exaratae Thomae Myriell A.D. 1616.* It consists of 90 anthems, 20 motets and 81 part-songs, written mainly by English composers, famous and obscure, but with a liberal sprinkling of Italians as well. Perhaps the most noteworthy manuscript of this period containing a single work is Egerton 3512, of about 1610-16, which comprises the full score of Tallis's monumental forty-part motet *Spem in alium non habui*, with English words 'Sing and glorifie'.

An extensive anthology containing both vocal and instrumental music is a manuscript of over 1000 pages (Egerton 3665), almost certainly in the hand of Francis Tregian, a recusant musician, who died in 1619. (The hand is identical with that of the Fitzwilliam Virginal Book.) It comprises *Villanelle*, madrigals, motets and fancies, by more than 100 composers, mainly English or Italian. Its value lies in the fact that some of the printed sources are no longer extant. Among the great song-writers of the first half of the seventeenth century was Henry Lawes, who compiled a large collection (53723) of 325 songs and dialogues, spanning over two decades, from before 1630 to after 1650. (This is one of the largest autograph volumes of its kind.) Among his single songs is one of unusual character, entitled *London's farwell to ye parliament* (32343, ff.11,12): twenty verses and the melody at the head are all in Lawes's hand. The important Sloane manuscript (1021), the commonplace book of Johann Stobaeus already mentioned, contains, ff.51-88 *passim*, a score of German songs, many of them probably composed by him.

From the mid-seventeenth century onwards there is a steady increase in the quantity of viol music, by such composers as John Jenkins, William Lawes and Simon Ives. One manuscript (31423, ff.1-75v), for example, consists almost entirely of three-part fantasies by Jenkins; another set (18940-44) contains airs and dances in four parts, with a harpsichord part, including pieces by all three composers. In the field of sacred music the collections have numerous services and anthems by such musicians as George Jeffries and Pelham Humfrey. But these are over-shadowed by the genius of Henry Purcell, some of whose masterpieces are to be found in a single volume (30930). Here are anthems, In nomines, string fantasias (including on f.50 reversed, that 'on one note') the chaconne, two canons and Latin psalms. (This volume, which was written in 1680 and 1683, is similar to another 'fair-copy' autograph collection of Purcell in the Royal Music Library, mentioned on p.36.) Another notable Purcell autograph is *The Yorkshire Feast Song* of c.1689 (Egerton 2956).

Purcell's contemporaries included a number of Italians who settled in England. One was Pietro Reggio, quite a number of whose works, mostly in his hand, are in the collections. There are twenty-three Latin motets, with bass (31440, ff.67-73, 102v-173v), and, in the same manuscript (f.181), a canon *Non nobis, Domine*, for 120 voices, and a dialogue for five voices, (ff.131v-140v), sung by Abraham, Isaac, Angel, and a chorus, to an Italian text *Splendea qual viuo sole*. Among foreign manuscripts of this period are a volume of Italian cantatas and songs (27931) written for a member of the Medici family: the composer is G. P. Colonna (d.1695), and the autograph of Carissimi's motet *Audite, sancti* (Harley 1501, f.48).

Copies of Purcell's anthems are to be found in many collections of English church music made late in the seventeenth century and early in the eighteenth. The most remarkable collection of this period was begun in 1715 by Thomas Tudway, Professor of Music at Cambridge. He entitled the first volume thus: *A collection of the most celebrated Services and Anthems used in the Church of England from the Reformation to the Restauration of K. Charles II. Composed by the best masters.* Gradually, Tudway extended his anthology until it ran to six volumes (Harley 7337-42), the last of which he finished in 1720. From Tallis, Byrd and Gibbons, Tudway ranged through the seventeenth century, including Blow and Purcell, John Bowman, Thomas Roseingrave and William Croft. Tudway also included some anthems of his own, and three by his contemporary Maurice Greene. Twenty-eight of the latter's anthems, some in his autograph, are in a miscellaneous volume (17850, ff.38v-20v).

The name which soon overshadowed all English music of his generation is that of Handel, the bulk of whose autographs are, as already mentioned (p.37), in the Royal Music Library. There is, however, an important residue in the Department of Manuscripts. Perhaps the best known works are the three organ concertos no.2-4 of op.4, of 1735. There are also two movements of a concerto, c.1715 (30310, ff.52-62), both of which occur, differently scored, in the *Water Music*. Of Handel's sacred vocal works, there are the eighth Chandos anthem, *As pants the Hart* (30308, ff.17-27), and an 'Allelujah' chorus (King's 317, ff.33-37) which he added in 1735 to his organ concerto in F (op.4), for performance at the end of *Il trionfo del tempo e della verità*, when it was revived in 1737.

The two secular vocal autographs are the cantata *Lungi dal mio bel nume*, of 1708 (30310, ff.2-12v), and the score of a selection (30310, ff.13-38) from an unperformed opera written in 1750, known variously as *Alcides* or *Alceste*. Operas bulk large in the Granville collection of Handel manuscripts (Egerton 2910-46). Mostly written by the composer's amanuensis John Christopher Smith the elder, this collection includes sixteen operas and eight oratorios and many other major vocal and instrumental works. Another Egerton manuscript, 2953, is a score, in Smith's hand, of *Acige e Galatea*, which includes four leaves in the composer's hand that are missing from the autograph in the Royal Music Library.

In connection with Handel's operas, and the broadly Italianate taste of his time, it may be mentioned here that the collections contain three important manuscript records of performance. There is a 'List of dramas of Italian opera, acted in England', between 1705 and 1776, with the names of the singers and dates (Burney 5120). For the Italian operas given at the Haymarket Theatre in London, Francis Colman compiled 'Opera registers from 1712 to 1734', with names (11258, ff.18v-32), and for Drury Lane Theatre, there are papers relating to its accounts from 1714 to 1717, signed by its managers, Colley Cibber, Robert Wilks, and Barton Booth (Egerton 2159, ff.15-40).

An important manuscript of Heinrich Schütz, in a copyist's hand, consists of the organ part of his setting of Psalms 119 and 100 and a Magnificat, with a printed title-page, dated 1671, reading: *Königs und Propheten Davids Hundert und Neunzehender Psalm . . . nebenst dem Anhange des 100. Psalms und eines Magnificat . . . Organum*, preceded by the composer's autograph dedication. (This manuscript forms part of Loan 77, a collection of some sixty autographs from the Stefan Zweig collection, deposited on loan by his heirs. The most important are mentioned singly or in groups later in these pages.)

The library owns only one original manuscript of Johann Sebastian Bach's, mostly in his autograph, namely that of the second book of *Das wohltemperirte Clavier*, the '48'. It came to the museum in 1896, as part of a bequest from Eliza Wesley. On loan (Loan 65, also from the Stefan Zweig collection), there are four musical autographs of J. S. Bach – the score of cantata no.5 *Wo soll ich fliehen hin*, composed for the 19th Sunday after Trinity (Loan 65/1): a viola part of cantata no.130 *Herr Gott, dich loben alle wir*; and a single leaf (Loan 65/3) bearing two chorales from the *Orgel-Büchlein*, BWV 631 and 632. Two interesting Bach association pieces are a manuscript copy of *Die Kunst der Fuge* owned by Brahms, and eight part books of choruses in the St. Matthew Passion said to have been used by Mendelssohn in the epoch-making performance that he gave in Berlin on 11 March 1829. Bach's sons Carl Philipp Emanuel, Wilhelm Friedemann, and Wilhelm Friedrich Ernst are all found in the collections, the last-named represented by a number of instrumental works in autograph.

A remarkable German manuscript from J. S. Bach's time is a collection of lute solos, written from 1717 to 1724 by Silvius Leopold Weiss, who was active at Dresden and other German courts. It contains 222 pieces, many of which are grouped into suites. From the later eighteenth century there date two large series of unaccompanied melodies of French songs, (Egerton 814-7, and Egerton 1519-21), the former compiled after 1744 and the latter after 1726. Both groups contain songs from operas set to new words, often of a scurrilous character, and 'chansons historiques' referring to historical events and persons connected with the French court from 1617 to 1726, and of a similar nature. Another French manuscript, of a slightly later period, is the autograph of six songs, with accompaniment for strings and basso continuo, by J. J. Rousseau.

The collections are rich in manuscript scores of operas and other vocal works by Italian composers, dating from the early 1700s onwards. Two of the names well represented from the first half of the century are Alessandro Scarlatti and Nicolo Porpora. Twenty of the latter's operas include the autographs of *Angelica*, 1714, *Siface*, c.1726, portions of *Mitridate*, 1733, *Polifemo*, 1734, *Ifigenia*, 1735, *Arianne e Teseo*, 1733 and Acts 2 and 3 of *Didone*, c.1740. Besides many of Porpora's songs, there are the autographs of part 2 of his cantata in honour of the Emperor Charles VI, 1712, and of two serenatas of 1736. Of Scarlatti there is in Loan 77 the autograph cantata *Ombre tacite e sole*, 1711, and among some twenty-five operas by him the autograph of *Griselda*, 1721: numerous duets and songs in contemporary copies attest the extent of his popularity. Some of these manuscripts are part of a remarkable collection of Italian music (14101-249), formed by Gaspar Selvaggi of Naples, and presented by the Marquis of Northampton in 1843. It comprises both sacred and secular music, including numerous operas, by nearly 100 composers, chiefly of the Neapolitan school, and dating from the early eighteenth century to the early nineteenth.

There is a considerable variety of other eighteenth century music such as *Sei sonate* for violin and bass, by the Neapolitan composer Emanuele Barbella, in autograph. Of Dimitri Bortniansky, whose early studies took him to Naples, there are the scores, in early manuscript copies, of three operas – *Alcide; azione teatrale*, 1778, *Le faucon*, 1786, and *Le fils rival*, 1787. A considerable number of operas by Cimarosa, and some volumes of separate arias by him, include a few in his hand. Some of these are in a large collection of Italian operas (15979-16160) formed by Dragonetti and bequeathed by him in 1846. It comprises works dating from the mid-eighteenth century to the early nineteenth. A volume of sixty-five Freemason's songs, in German (32596), includes one or two adapted to melodies by Mozart, and, while mentioning a few other – rather obscure – composers, gives for the majority only initials, in the wonted Masonic manner. As a rare example of a song by royalty may be mentioned the autograph of *Amour, fuis loin de moi* by Queen Marie Antoinette.

Gluck is represented by the autograph (Loan 77/27) of an aria *Misero! E che faro*, from his opera *Alceste*. The earliest autograph of any member of the Viennese school of composers is the score of Haydn's symphony no.40, in F, 1763. From 1766 dates the autograph of his E flat piano sonata (31273, ff.33-38v). The collections also include the autographs of Haydn's 'Drum Roll' symphony, in E flat, no.103, and three other 'Salomon' symphonies in loan collections – no.97, in C major (Loan 77/30), no.95, in C minor, and no.96, in D. The last two are bound with a manuscript copy of symphony no.98 in B flat and comprise the first volume of a set of four, in the Royal Philharmonic Society's library (Loan 4). The other three volumes contain the remaining nine 'Salomon' symphonies, all, like no.98, in manuscript scores written in London, on paper watermarked 1794, at the time of Haydn's visit. An opera by Haydn is the autograph of *Orlando Palladino*, 1782, Acts I and II only. Haydn's sacred music is represented in autograph by some sketches of 'Awake the harp' and 'The heav'ns are telling', two choruses in *The Creation* (28613, ff.2,3) and by two numbers, in score, of an intended oratorio composed in London c.1794, on a text by Marchamont Needham. The great Mass in D minor, composed in 1798, is found in a copy made after 1802 by Johannes Elssler, Haydn's amanuensis. An autograph duet of 1796, *Guarda qui che lo vedrai*, with piano accompaniment occurs in Additional 32173 (f.3). The same manuscript (ff.39,75) has the autograph of two sacred odes composed by Haydn's younger brother, Johann Michael, at Salzburg in 1778 and 1782.

The department has one of the best collections of Mozart autographs apart from those in his native Austria and in one or two libraries in Germany. The gem is undoubtedly the scores of his last ten string quartets – the six dedicated to Haydn, the so-called 'Hoffmeister' in D, K499, and the three written for the King of Prussia. These ten autographs were bequeathed in 1907 by Miss Harriet Chichele-Plowden. The others in the collections are, in the order of original Köchel numbers: K172, string quartet in B flat; K246, piano concerto in C, cadenzas to the first and second movements; K386, rondo in A for piano and orchestra, three leaves only (32181, ff.250-252v: originally mis-catalogued as by Süssmayr); K406, string quintet in C minor; K546, fugue in C minor for string quartet; piano sonata in B flat, K570, bars 65 to the end of the first movement. Besides these compositions there is the book of musical exercises written by Thomas Attwood (58437) when he was studying composition with Mozart in Vienna in 1785-86, notable for the fact that it contains numerous corrections and some completions in Mozart's hand, besides a few small pieces composed by him.

The department is also fortunate in having a collection of Mozart autographs deposited by the heirs of Stefan Zweig (Loan 42). The compositions, in Köchel-number order, are: K173, string quartet in D minor, last movement; K377, violin sonata in F; K408, march in C for orchestra; K447, concerto for horn and orchestra, in E flat; K476, *Das Veilchen*; K492, *Le nozze di Figaro*, 'Non so più'; K559,560a, canons; K609, five contredances for orchestra; K614, string quintet in E flat; K617, quintet for armonica, flute, oboe, viola and cello; K621, *La clemenza di Tito*, 'Deh prende un dolce amplesso'. The musical documents are: Mozart's own thematic catalogue of his compositions from February 1784 to November 1791; four letters to his cousin Maria Anna Thekla Mozart; his signed marriage contract, dated 3 August 1782.

The quantity of Beethoven autographs in the collections is far smaller. The only major complete work is the violin sonata in G, op.30, no.3, presented, like the Mozart quartets, by Miss Chichele-Plowden. A lesser piece is a portion of a mandoline sonata (29801, f.87). The same volume (f.1-2v) contains a cadenza to the rondo of Mozart's piano concerto in D minor. An unusual manuscript is the autograph draft of twelve airs for piano, with accompaniment for flute or violin, which were published in *Sechs variirte Themen*, op.105, and *Zehn variirte Themen*, op.107. The complete song *Lied aus der Ferne* is preserved together with autograph sketches for other works. Another interesting sketch (29987, ff.25, 26v) comprises arrangements of, or additional accompaniments to, portions of Handel's *Messiah*. The collections contain several sketch books, containing, among other drafts, sketches for the Pastoral symphony (31766, ff.1-48v), and piano trios op.70, nos.1,2, for several quartets (29997), for *The Ruins of Athens* and *King Stephen*, and for various piano works (29801). These, and sketches in other manuscripts and printed and manuscript copies with the composer's notes or corrections, are all described in *Beethoven and England* by Pamela Willetts (see p.44), which also lists all the letters, relics, etc. that are in the collections.

The most important of the autographs of Schubert is his piano sonata in G, op.78 (D894), 1826, given by Johann Ernst Perabo (d.1920), an American pianist of German birth. The rest of Perabo's collection was presented by one of his pupils, Edward Perry Warren. It included the autograph score of the Mass in B flat, op.141 (D324), and five songs, *Der Fischer, Wandrers Nachtlied*, three Italian songs (D225, 224,902) and a fragment – the last two leaves – of *Die Sehnsucht* (D636). The bequest of E. H. W. Meyerstein (who was once on the staff of the Department of Manuscripts) included Schubert's *Morgenlied* and *Abendlied* (D266,276), sketches for two sections of *Stabat Mater* (D383), and another song *Namenstagslied*, (D695). Another – underrated – aspect of Schubert's genius is seen in the autograph score of his one-act opera *Die Verschworenen: oder die häusliche Krieg* of 1823.

More autographs by Haydn, Beethoven and Schubert are found in Loan 77. It includes the score of Haydn's piano trio in E flat minor (after 1795), a sketch of the second movement of his string quartet op.76 no.3 and the score of the symphony in C, no.97. The works by Beethoven are: sketches for the last movement of the cello sonata op.69, and for

Clärchen's song 'Die Trommel gerühret' in the music to *Egmont*; the score of no.6, 'Harmonie auf dem Theater' in the music to *The Ruins of Athens*; the song *Der Kuss*, op.128; and the second setting of the canon *Kurz ist der Schmerz*, WoO 166. Of Schubert, there are the song *An die Musik*, D547b, and the scores of two other late vocal works – *Mirjams Siegesgesang*, D942, and *Schlachtlied*, D912. His instrumental autographs are piano works – three German dances D146 no.2, D783 nos.1,2, and D769 no.2. There is also the autograph of an aria from Metastasio's *Demofoonte*, D42.

The three Weber autographs are all instrumental works – the variations, op.6, 1804, for piano trio on Vogler's song *Woher mag das wohl kommen* in the Perabo collection; the piano concerto op.11, 1810, bequeathed by Meyerstein; and the trio for piano, flute and cello, op.63, 1819. Two other manuscripts, both contemporary copies, are connected with Weber's visit to London in 1826. The score of the three-act opera *Oberon* is the one used when the work was produced at Covent Garden, perhaps for the premiere on 26 April. It was bequeathed by Sir George Smart in whose house Weber died on 5 June. This score has some notes and corrections in Weber's writing. A score of his *Jubel-Ouverture*, 1818, (in the Royal Philharmonic Society's library) has a title-page in his hand, dedicated to the Society which gave the first performance in England in 1826.

From the eighteenth to the mid-nineteenth century one of the focal points of musical life in London was the pleasure gardens. Much music composed for Vauxhall has survived in manuscript. By the prolific James Hook there are cantatas with orchestra (19647, ff.1-14v,90-101v) of 1783, others of 1800 (28971, ff.106-124), and a chorus of 1800 (28791, ff.102-105v), also with orchestra. All these are in his autograph. So too is a 'New Catch' for seven voices, 1786, with orchestra (19647, f.15), and *I'll give you a toast*, 1798, for three voices (19647, f.102). This manuscript contains eleven orchestral songs for Vauxhall; there are fifty-five more, 1800-1803, in 28971. Nine others (34007, ff.46-84) date from 1804. Many of the original singers are named in these autographs. A manuscript dating from c.1750 to c.1770 includes songs for both Vauxhall and Ranelagh, by John Worgan, Samuel Howard and Charles Dibdin (38488A, ff.220v-234). (There are numerous other songs by Dibdin, mostly in his hand, especially those for his 'Table Entertainments' – eg 30951-55.) The later years of Vauxhall are represented by two autograph collections of glees and songs written for it by Sir Henry Bishop from 1830 to 1834 (36966-68), with elaborate orchestral accompaniments. Another interesting sequence of English manuscripts (49624-7) comprises the autograph scores of twenty-three symphonies written from 1760 to 1764, at various towns in Yorkshire, by William – later, as Astronomer Royal, Sir William – Herschel.

The notable recorders of musical history in England, who together spanned nearly seven decades, were William Ayrton (1777-1858) and Sir George Smart (1776-1867). The first collection of Ayrton papers (52334-58) includes correspondence relating to the King's Theatre of which he was musical director and to the Coronation Festival of 1838; letters from musicians (Meyerbeer, Mendelssohn, etc.); papers relating to the Beethoven Quartet Society. In the second collection, the items of musical interest are in 60370, 60374-380, and include some lectures which Ayrton gave at the Royal Institution, after 1816.

Smart's collections (see also p.47) relate not only to his work in England but also to his European travels, from which his *Journals* have been published. He compiled a list (34278) of London and provincial festivals and concerts in which he was interested, either as conductor or composer, from 1798 to 1855. A collection of his papers (41771-9) comprises his correspondence mainly relating to the Philharmonic Society, 1790-1867; his comments on its concerts, 1813-60; bills of performances which he attended on his tour to Germany in 1825; and documents relating to Weber's only visit to England in 1826 and to his death in Smart's house. (The last group includes two printed bills of performance, with separate words, on 26 May 1826, of *Festival of Peace*, Weber's own arrangement of his *Jubel-Kantate.*) Smart also kept a memoranda book (42225), from 1793 to 1863.

Though Mendelssohn's autographs are relatively few, all exemplify his beautifully controlled calligraphy. The organ score of his anthem *Why, O Lord, delay for ever* (1840, op.96) is followed by an orchestral arrangement. A wordless canon (35026, f.66) is inscribed by the composer 'London, 7th Sept. 1837'. One of his best known works, the music for *A Midsummer Night's Dream*, is represented by his own piano arrangement, 1844, of the Scherzo, Notturno and Wedding March. The Meyerstein bequest included the autograph of the *Variations sérieuses.* A fugue in D minor for organ (14396, ff.33-34) was written by Mendelssohn at Berlin in 1833, for Vincent Novello, who presented the volume containing it to the British Museum. The sole chamber work is the string quartet in E flat, composed, without opus number, in 1823. The collections contain a number of his letters, of which two (38091, ff.45-9) were written to William Bartholomew about *Elijah*, in 1846, when the oratorio was first heard at the Birmingham Festival. The same work is the subject of more correspondence with Bartholomew, who translated it into English, and received eleven letters from Mendelssohn (47859A).

Rossini's operas are found only in contemporary, though fairly early, copies. There is a version of *Mosé in Egitto*, as an oratorio (before 1841), and *Demetrio e Polibio, Elizabetta, Regina d'Inghilterra, L'inganno felice* (prepared for a London performance in 1837, with two additional songs), *La donna del lago, Semiramide* and *Otello* are among the full scores in the collections. Vocal works in Rossini's autograph are *Stabat Mater*, c.1841, a song *Conçois tu toutes mes douleurs* (45102E, ff.19,20v; f.18 of this volume being his signed certificate, 1861, for Mme Doti to sing in his *Stabat Mater*), and three secular works (together comprising 30246) – a quartet *Dall'oriente*, 1823, an undated trio *In giorno si bello*, and a song *Il pianto delle muse in morte di Lord Byron*, 1824. There are also some letters in his hand.

Of Bellini's operas only two are in the collections, in manuscript scores of uncertain date. That of *Il Pirata* includes some unusual instruments – tromboncino, serpents and harmonica, and serpents are also found in a score of *Adelson e Salvini.* Donizetti is represented by scores of *Anna Bolena, Il Furioso, Lucia di Lammermor, Le convenienze ed inconvenienze teatrali*, and *L'Elisir d'amore* – all apparently used for unidentified but fairly early productions. Pride of place for Verdi must be given to the autograph of *Attila.* Other full scores in contemporary copies, mostly associated with the London productions given by Mapleson, are *I due Foscari, Ernani, Rigoletto, Les vèpres siciliennes,* and *Il trovatore.* Another vocal work in Verdi's hand is the full score of the *Inno alle nazioni,* written for the opening of the London Exhibition of 1862. The autograph simply bears the word 'Cantica'.

The department's own collections include one manuscript in Wagner's hand – a sketch of the 'people's chorus' from Act II of *Rienzi* (Egerton 2746, ff.3,3v). There are also some Wagner autographs in Loan 77, of which the most important are three pieces from *Der fliegende Holländer* – the revised full score of the final section of the overture, the close of Act III in full score, and a copy of the overture with some corrections in the composer's hand. Besides a few letters, this Loan has some sketches of early works, among them the first movement of the C major symphony, arranged by the composer for piano duet. Of Meyerbeer there are two fragmentary autographs – an additional air in *Les Huguenots* (Egerton 2829, ff.6-9), and part of the overture to *Struensee* (35026, f.57), signed by the composer London, July 1855; two leaves in a copyist's score of *Jephtas Gelübde* (29906, ff.320v, 321), which apparently date from 1813, and also have expression marks throughout in the composer's hand. Of numerous operas by English nineteenth century composers, the best known are probably those by Balfe, nearly all in his autograph, and among them, *The Bohemian Girl.*

European operetta is represented by the score of Offenbach's *Fantasio*, 1872, largely in his hand; while of Sullivan there are the autograph full scores of *Patience* and *The Gondoliers.* An early instrumental autograph of Sullivan's is an 'Allegro risoluto' in B flat minor for piano, of 1866 (49977N).

Outside the field of opera, there is a fair sprinkling of autographs by the romantic composers. Chopin – a sketch for the mazurka in C, op.56, no.2, 1843 (47861A(i)), the two polonaises, op.40, and (both in Loan 77) the *Barcarolle*, and the mazurka, op.59, no.3: Schumann – the piano sonata in F minor op.14, 1836, and a march in B flat, op.76, no.2: Liszt – the oratorio *Christus*, an arrangement, 1877, for piano of his string quartet 'Angelus' (34182, ff.112-113v), the 'Czardas macabre' and 'Reminiscences de Boccanegra' (Egerton 2735, ff.9-264): Brahms – rhapsody in E flat, op.119, no.4, and (both in Loan 77) sketches for the last three movements of the second piano concerto, and the *Zigeunerlieder*, op.103: Dvořák – cello concerto in A, 1865, with piano accompaniment, and *Hymnus* op.30 (Loan 69): Gounod – *Messe solennelle de Sainte Cécile*, motet *O salutaris hostia*, and (in Loan 69) *Marche nuptiale* 1 and 2, and *Holy Vision* for baritone and orchestra, 1887: Lvov – the melody of the Russian national anthem, *Boze charya chranie*, with figured bass (copy made by Lvov in 1858; 37425, f.135): Borodin – draft of the *Petite suite* and draft of the Scherzo in A flat, both for piano: Mussorgsky, two songs of 1866 (both in Loan 77), *Iz slyoz moikh* and *Svetik Savishna*; Grieg – women's chorus *Foran sydens Kloster* with soprano and alto solo, op.20, c.1871.

From this period there dates a remarkable album, kept by Eliza Wesley (daughter of Samuel Wesley) in London from 1836 to 1895 (35026). Besides small pieces by composers resident or visiting, it includes signatures and scraps of music by many famous musicians such as Grisi, Joachim, Lind, Clara Schumann, Tamberlik, Tamburini, and Verdi.

The representation of foreign composers of the later nineteenth century who lived well into the twentieth is very diverse. The autographs of Richard Strauss begin with a number of youthful works, including the string quartet op.2, the violin concerto op.8, the symphony op.12, a piano quartet op.13, and four groups of songs, op.19, 21, 29, 32 and 36. (All these are deposited on loan by Universal Edition.) The department owns what is perhaps his most famous song, *Ständchen*, and two pages of *Capriccio*, not found in the final version of the opera. Of Debussy there is a fragment in his hand from the uncompleted opera *La chute de la maison Usher*; an unusual autograph associated with him is Nijinsky's choreographic score of the ballet to *L'après-midi d'un faune.* An opera in the autograph of a lesser German composer, Erich Korngold, is *Der Ring des Polykrates,* op.7, 1916. The prolific Massenet, many of whose printed operatic full scores feature in the Music Library, is represented by a manuscript copy of *Le roi de Lahore*, of 1877. A gift from Dohnányi's widow has provided two groups of his autographs. One comprises juvenile works – piano and chamber music, songs, and sacred pieces – ranging from 1888 to 1893: the other, mature compositions, such as the second piano concerto and second violin concerto, which cover the years from 1940 to about 1960. Another gift, from Dohnányi's sister, included a fragment of the finale of the E minor piano concerto.

Loan 77 includes autographs by major European composers, largely of works dating from the early decades of the twentieth century. These are: Mahler's *Urlicht*, for voice and orchestra, 1893; nos.1,3,4 and 5 (bars 1-17 only) of Schoenberg's Five orchestral pieces, op.16 (1909); the full score of Webern's Six pieces for orchestra, op.4 (later op.6, 1909); the full score of Bartok's Four pieces for orchestra, op.12 (1912, orchestrated 1921); the short score of the first and last movement of Hindemith's *Kammermusik* no.2, op.36, no.1 (1924); Ravel's two-piano arrangement (1930) of his Bolero (1928); the prologue to Berg's *Lulu* (1934), in score.

The sole American composer of the later nineteenth century is Macdowell, the autograph of whose *Ländliche Suite für grosses Orchester*, op.37, was presented by his widow in both full score and in his arrangement for piano duet. The sole Stravinsky autograph owned by the library is the full score of his *Capriccio* for piano and orchestra, of 1929, presented by Mrs Kate Henriette Roth. The only autograph of Hindemith's (included in the Boult papers: see p.105) is his *Trauermusik* for viola and strings which he composed in London on the occasion of George V's death in 1936, himself playing the solo part at the first performance. Karg-Elert's partita in E for organ, op.100, is accompanied by some of his letters to Godfrey Sceats. The Galliard collection includes a few small pieces in the autograph by Moszkowski, Reinecke, Reger and Ornstein. Among other autographs by foreign composers are *A Room*, a piano piece by John Cage, 1943, and another by Pizzetti, headed 'Dalle melodie di un vecchio auleta', 1909.

A collection of manuscripts deposited by J. and W. Chester/Wilhelm Hansen (Loan 75) includes a number of important autographs by Falla, *Amor brujo*, piano score, and *El retablo de Maese Pedro*, vocal score; Poulenc, *Histoire de Babar*; Rachmaninov, piano concerto no.3, op.30; Stravinsky, *Renard*, full score, *Trois histoires pour enfants*, for voice and piano, and no.1 of the same for voice and orchestra, *Pulcinella*, vocal score, Suite no.2 for small orchestra. Autographs of English composers in this collection include Constant Lambert's *Elegiac Blues* and *Eight Poems of Li Po*.

The collection of autographs by most of the major English composers of the twentieth century, including those whose work began in the later part of the nineteenth, is remarkably comprehensive. This is due to the intensification of the policy begun in the nineteenth century, that the British Museum should build up the manuscript sources of the country's music. (A similar plan has been followed by the national library — or equivalent institutions — of most countries: hence, for example, the scarcity of Bruckner manuscripts outside Austria.) In the case of England this policy was enhanced, from the turn of the nineteenth century onwards, by the emergence of some composers of internationally recognized stature.

There is a small number of Stanford's autographs. They comprise his 'Irish' symphony, the setting of Tennyson's poem *The Revenge*; two fugues for piano, two pieces for alto and piano, op.160; and three works in the Galliard collection — the organ sonata in F, op.149, 1917; the piano trio no.3, op.158, 1918; and 'scènes de ballet', op.150, 1917; The Elgar collection, on the other hand, is extensive, thanks largely to the generosity of his daughter, Mrs. Carice Elgar Blake, who deposited several large groups of her father's autographs on loan, and then converted these loans into outright gifts. There are eighty-five volumes of these autographs, both completed works and sketches. They may be described in three groups. The major works are the symphony in A flat, the 'Enigma' variations, *The Apostles, The Kingdom* (vocal score), the violin concerto, the piano quintet, *Sea Pictures*, two Pomp and Circumstance Marches, op.39 no.1 and no.4, the Introduction and Allegro for strings, and the overture *Cockaigne*. The lesser works include *Sospiri*, the Romance for bassoon and orchestra, *From the Bavarian Highlands*, the organ sonata op.28, and *Carillon*. There are also an extensive quantity of songs and ten early works for wind quintet. A gift of eleven autograph scores from Messrs. Elkin & Co. included some theatrical music, notably *The Starlight Express* and *The Sanguine Fan*. From the BBC came the sketches for the third symphony first deposited on loan in 1935, and presented outright in 1969.

Because of the concentration of Delius's autographs in the Delius Trust, there are relatively few elsewhere. The British Library has *An Arabesk*, the Requiem and the score of *Fennimore and Gerda* (these lent by Universal Edition); a dance for harpsichord, and two leaves of the incidental music for *Hassan*. Among all the English composers of this generation the one most completely represented in the collections is Vaughan Williams, thanks largely to the munificence of his widow, Ursula Vaughan Williams. Her several gifts cover every group in his entire output, from *The Robin's Nest*, a piano piece of 1878, his sixth year, through his whole life, right up to the ninth symphony of 1956-57. The chief autographs in score in the principal categories are: symphonies – the 'Pastoral', no.5 in D, no.9 in E minor; concertos – piano, oboe, harmonica (romance), tuba; music for the stage – *Sir John in Love, The Poisoned Kiss, Riders to the Sea, The Pilgrim's Progress*: vocal music – *Towards the unknown Region, Sancta civitas, Hodie*; film music – *Coastal Command, 49th Parallel, The England of Elizabeth*. Gifts from Ursula Vaughan Williams also comprise many early and unpublished works (57265-95), among them the music for the Abinger Pageant (with notes by E. M. Forster) and folk-song arrangements (59535-6). In all, this collection amounts to over 160 volumes. Gifts of Vaughan Williams autographs from other donors include the full scores of *Job*, the sixth and eighth symphonies, A Sea Symphony, the London Symphony (reconstructed by the composer and others from the parts), *Scott of the Antarctic, Hugh the Drover* in vocal score, and *The Lark ascending* in piano and violin reduction. Full scores of the fourth symphony and the *Concerto accademico* were acquired by purchase, and that of the *Sinfonia antartica* is in the Royal Philharmonic Society's loan collection. A large quantity of sketches for compositions of all kinds and periods rounds off the whole.

Most of the autographs of Gustav Holst are comprised in a gift made in 1952 by his widow Mrs. Isobel Holst, and Miss Imogen Holst, his daughter. Now bound in thirty-five volumes, it consists mostly of unpublished compositions, but includes such notable works as *The Mystic Trumpeter* and the Cotswolds Symphony, besides a quantity of sketches. Holst autographs from other sources are a first sketch, in condensed score, of the *Choral Fantasia*, six songs to words by Humbert Wolfe, and 'Dawn' from *Hymns from the Rig Veda*. A later collection of Holst autographs (57863-910), presented by various donors, comprises a quantity of early works, written before 1895, and a substantial number of later ones, such as the scores of *Beni Mora*, the Fugal Overture, *Egdon Heath*, and the Double Concerto, and of *The Perfect Fool, At the Boar's Head*, and the *Hymn of Jesus* (all partly autograph). There are also various sketch-books.

A substantial collection of Rutland Boughton, now in seventy-three volumes, was presented in 1962 by his son and daughter. It covered every phase of his musical activity, including, among the ten music dramas, the full score of *The Immortal Hour*; among the orchestral works, his two oboe concertos; and among chamber music, two string quartets and an oboe quartet. Percy Grainger's widow, Ella Grainger, gave a substantial quantity of his autographs, including some of his best known works – *Hill Song I* and *II, Mock Morris*, and some *British Folk Music Settings*, among them *Shepherd's Hey* and *Country Gardens.*

John Ireland's autographs were secured for the collections by a gift from Mrs. Norah Kathleen Kirby. The thirty volumes include his best known orchestral compositions, *The Forgotten Rite, Mai Dun*, the *Satyricon* overture, and his piano concerto. There are also the score of his music for the film, *The Overlanders*, many piano pieces and songs and sketch-books. For the autographs of Sir Arnold Bax, the library was indebted to Harriet Cohen, who gave a small group in 1960, and deposited two large ones on loan four years later: the latter were converted into outright gifts in 1969. The seventy-seven resultant volumes show the full range of Bax's work – four of his first six symphonies in full score, the concertos for violin and for cello, many other orchestral works, including *The Tale the Pine Trees knew*, much music for groups, piano works, and songs. One of Sir Arthur Bliss's best-known works is the music to the ballet *Check-Mate*, and this is his sole autograph score in the collections. Nearly as slender is the tally of Sir William Walton's music: it comprises the *Te Deum* (composed for the coronation of Queen Elizabeth II), presented by himself; a fanfare composed for the Nato Parliamentarians' Conference held in London, 1959; a draft score of the Polka from *Façade*; and two pieces dating from 1916, his fourteenth year. Havergal Brian presented a number of his symphonies – nos.7 to 13, in full score, no.5 in vocal score, and sketches of no.6 in vocal score, and the *Symphonia Tragica* in full score. These he gave in 1963, and in 1967 the full scores of symphony no.27 and the sinfonia in C minor.

In the case of Sir Michael Tippett, the British Library now owns a high proportion of all his major works in autograph. The scores of *The Midsummer Marriage* and *King Priam* were acquired individually, while *The Ice Break* and *The Knot Garden* were among some forty autographs which the Library purchased from Sir Michael himself in 1980. They cover over four decades of his output, and include the four symphonies, *A Child of our Time*, the concerto for double string orchestra, and the first string quartet in its final version. Its first version was among the Macnaughton Concerts Collection, acquired in 1976, in which there was a considerable variety of autographs by British musicians, such as the voice-parts of Britten's *A Boy was born*, the first draft of Elizabeth Lutyens' *Time off? Not a ghost of a chance*, and pieces by Roger Smalley, Tim Souster, John McCabe, and Peter Maxwell Davies.

Among miscellaneous monographs of this period may be mentioned Roberto Gerhard's *Allegories* and his Concerto for orchestra, both composed in England after he became a British subject. Another, on a totally different level, is Dame Myra Hess's immensely popular piano arrangement of Bach's *Jesu Joy of Man's Desiring* (1926, 57486M). In lighter vein are two autographs of H. Fraser-Simson, the score of his incidental music to A. A. Milne's *Toad of Toad Hall*, and his setting of poems from *When we were very young*.

After Benjamin Britten's death in 1976, the British Library was able to acquire some thirty of his scores in lieu of estate duty. (Only microfilms are kept in the Department of Manuscripts: the originals are on loan to the Britten-Pears Library in Aldeburgh.) The most notable autographs available on film are the *Sinfonietta* op.1, the *Phantasy Quartet*, op.2, *Variations on a theme of Frank Bridge*, the short score of the *Serenade for tenor, horn and strings, The Beggar's Opera* (mostly in Britten's hand), *Canticle II Abraham and Isaac*, the *Third Suite* for cello, op.87, the *Third String Quartet* op.94, and the incidental music to the play *The Ascent of F6*, by Auden and Isherwood. There are on film five major works in short score which are entirely autograph – *The Turn of the Screw, Midsummer Night's Dream*, the *War Requiem*, the *Cello Symphony* and *Curlew River*. (Their full scores also, partly autograph, are in the film collection.) Besides these, the department owns the autograph full score of *Gloriana* (given to it by the Britten-Pears Library), partly in Imogen Holst's hand.

These last few pages afford only a selection – which may perhaps seem arbitrary – from a great quantity of music by some English composers who were active from the late nineteenth century onwards. (The names of many others will be found in the index to the Willetts supplement to Hughes-Hughes and in other departmental sources.) But it may serve to indicate the wealth and variety of what has been preserved in autograph for posterity.

Theory

The manuscripts of musical theory are remarkably varied, and date back, in terms of some of the original texts, almost to the origins of the subject in Western Europe: they provide a fair sample of its development up to the middle of the nineteenth century. The following is only a selection from some 250 items listed in this category, which includes works by some of the most significant classical and mediaeval theorists.

There are texts (19353, ff.2-32v) of the *Harmonikai stoecheiai* of Aristoxenos (4th cent. BC), and (27863, ff.108-

21) of the *Eisagoge harmonike* of Cleonides (fl. 2nd cent. AD). These are matched by a text (19353, ff.237-54v) of the *Musike eisagoge* of Alypius (fl. 3rd cent. AD), and of the *Peri mousikes* (Harley 5691, 94-133v) of Aristides Quintilianus (fl. 3rd or 4th cent. AD), books 1, 2 and part of book 3. All these four manuscripts were written in the sixteenth century.

Of a number of manuscripts of the *De musica* of Boethius, the earliest complete text (Arundel 77, ff.6v-62) is of the eleventh century, while some imperfect extracts, written in the tenth century, comprise Harley 3595. There are a dozen manuscripts containing various treatises by Guido d'Arezzo, the earliest being a volume in the Additional series (17808), written in the eleventh century, probably in France. It contains his *Micrologus, Regulae rhythmicae*, and other works.

In Cotton Vespasian A.ii ff.131-138b there is an important treatise, dating from the twelfth to thirteenth century, which deals with the essentials of music as then practised, solmization, syllables, division of the monochord, intervals, and the like. With the incipit 'Musica Johannis', the manuscript comprised 27 chapters, but breaks off in chapter 12. The author, formerly presumed from mistaken external evidence, to be an English monk named John Cotton, is now generally identified with Johannes of Affligem (fl.1100), a theorist probably from Lorraine or Flanders. Lansdowne 763 is an English manuscript of the fifteenth century, bearing on f.2 the name of John Wylde, who worked at Waltham Abbey from about 1420 to 1450. Though not now thought to be the author of any of the twenty treatises in this manuscript, Wylde is important as the editor and copyist who preserved some unique sources of information regarding faburden and descant.

A notable Italian manuscript of the late fifteenth century (22315) includes (ff.1-60) one of the two known sources for the treatise beginning 'Praefatio libelli musicalis de ritu canendi vetustissino et novo', by Johannes Legrense generally known, as here, as Johannes Gallicus. (This manuscript has an additional interest in that it is in the hand of Legrense's pupil Nicolaus Burtius, himself a noted musical theorist.) The second source for the treatise is Harley 6525, likewise of the late fifteenth century, which is also a unique source for two other treatises by Legrense, 'Praefatiuncula in . . . tacitam . . . numerorum concinentiam', and 'Tacita . . . stupendaque numerorum, musica'. A manuscript in the early Additional series (4911), dating from the early sixteenth century, is of interest as being written by an unknown Scotsman. It bears a title 'The Art of Music collecit out of all Ancient Doctovris of Music'. Its three books include quotations of music or texts from Josquin, the *Micrologus* of Ornithoparcus (printed 1517), Gafori, Wollick and other composers or theoreticians of the Renaissance.

An anonymous English manuscript of the early seventeenth century (Royal 18 B. xix) is entitled 'The Praise of Musicke . . . and the necessarye vse of it in ye service & Christian Churche of God', and deals with such topics as 'The occasions of the decay of Musick in Cathedrall & Colledge Churches', which were causing concern at that time. Another anonymous manuscript (Harley 4160), dating from the very end of the seventeenth century includes (f.29) 'An account of the King of France['s] Water-works' at Versailles, where in May 1698 the King, Louis XIV, showed them (and their musical capacities) to the British Ambassador, William Bentinck, first Earl of Portland, and (f.33), 'The way of making an artificial nightingale, as it is in water-works'. From about the same time is a short treatise written by John Blow (but not in his autograph), 'Rules for playing of a Thorough-Bass upon Organ and Harpsecon' (34072, ff.1-5).

One of the most substantial collections of English writings about music is that comprised in eight volumes, mostly in the hand of the Hon. Roger North (c.1651-1734). Besides his autobiography – delightfully entitled 'Notes of Me' – and reminiscences, he left copious essays on harmony, acoustics, aesthetics, performance and the like. The anthology *Roger North on Music* (Novello, 1959, edited by John Wilson) includes his most important writings, but there remains in these manuscripts (32506, 32531-37) a good deal that still merits study.

A substantial manuscript (6137), of 360 folios, comprises a history of musical theory, finely written, with a title-page reading *Traité de l'harmonie des sens et de leurs rapports, ou la Musique theorique et pratique ancienne et moderne . . . par . . . Charles Hebert* and dated 1733. The author describes himself as 'Lecteur honoraire de philosophie dans l'université de Boulogne' (ie Bologna). The manuscript has a frontispiece, and other illustrations engraved after Domenico Mario Fratta, a Bolognese artist. There are plates with well drawn musical instruments. Apart from a brief mention in Eitner (derived from Oliphant), Hebert is not known to any standard work of musical reference, or to the catalogue of the Bibliothèque nationale. This manuscript seems to have escaped the notice of musical historiographers.

As an example of an autograph written for teaching purposes, there is a section of Tartini's *Trattato di musica secondo la vera scienzia dell' armonia*, 1754, entitled 'Regola del terzo suono' (32150, ff.2-16v) which he copied in about 1760 for his pupil J. G. Naumann. The latter wrote exercises on ff.9-11, which bear some corrections in Tartini's hand. Hieronymus Payer, a little known Viennese conductor, pianist and composer, wrote a considerable number of vocal and instrumental works. He also essayed an ambitious treatise, *Practische Methode zum* [sic] *Erlernung der musikalische Composition*, of which the autograph (32412, ff.54-207) is dated 1826. It was planned in three sections, 'Harmonie', 'Melodie', 'Melodie und Harmonie', but of these only the first is present. The expatriate English composer R. L. Pearsall wrote two substantial works of musical theory, *Observations on chanting*, 1851 (37490), and *Psalmodia or an essay on Psalmtunes*, 1842 (38549), both of interest for the study of nineteenth century practice.

Catalogues

There are some notable catalogues, of two kinds. The thematic catalogues include one of the compositions of the prolific eighteenth century flautist J. J. Quantz (32148). It was compiled about 1883 from various German sources by Carli Zoeller. Early in the nineteenth century Johann Anton André drew up a catalogue of all Mozart's works (32142) written before February 1784 (the date when he commenced his own *Verzeichnis*: see p.76). André used important primary sources, and prefaced his catalogue with some penetrating remarks (the earliest made) on the nature of Mozart's autographs. Among catalogues of musical libraries, there is one which describes Haydn's collection, compiled by Johann Elssler (32070), his amanuensis, about 1803. The first of the three sections lists printed music, both Haydn's own, and 160 items by other composers, including 29 publications dedicated to him. The second is of manuscript compositions, both his own and some 60 by others, including J. S. Bach, Handel, Muffat and Caldara. It also includes works of theory and musical history, by such writers as Fux, Mattheson and Marpurg and Burney (a copy of his *General History*). The last section lists Haydn's own autograph manuscripts. A notable English catalogue is that of Charles Burney's collection of musical literature (18191), drawn up in 1814: part of it was ultimately acquired by the British Museum. Royal taste is reflected in the catalogue of the large music library owned by King George V of Hanover (57974-5). A substantial catalogue of the twentieth century is that of the printed music and musical literature (54177) owned by George Hart, presumably the son of the distinguished violin maker and dealer who wrote successful books on this instrument. The binding, dated 1903, bears his name.

Iconography

The following Additional manuscripts contain portraits of musicians:

25176
- f.40 Georg Volcamer (Volcmar), engraving, 1623.

29804
- f.17 Weber, engraving.
- f.34 Rossini, engraving.

33965
- f.74 Henry Phillips, pen and ink portrait by Malibran.
- f.75 William Mutlow, organist of Gloucester Cathedral, pen and ink caricature by Malibran. [1832].

f.106	Charles de Bériot, pen and ink portrait by Malibran (?).
f.113v	Berlioz, lithograph.
f.119	Boieldieu, lithograph by L. M.
f.122	Boieldieu, stipple engraving by [A.] Wachsmann.
f.152	Halévy, lithograph.
f.186	William Cramer, engraving by T. Bragg after G. Place.
f.192	S. Dessauer, lithograph by Kriehuber. 1831.
35027	
f.3	'Master Samuel Wesley' photograph of a painting of him as a child.
f.8	Thomas Adams, photograph of a painting.
f.9	William Crotch, lithograph after W. Derby.
f.9	Tobias Langton, mezzotint by Faber after Nathaniel Tucker.
f.10	Thomas Augustine Arne, lithograph after Bartolozzi. 1782.
f.10v	Charles Dibdin. Engraving.
f.11	Samuel Arnold, engraving after [? John] Russell. 1790.
f.14	William Jackson of Exeter, engraving after J. Walker. 1819.
f.15	Thomas Attwood, lithograph.
f.17	Sir H. R. Bishop, engraving by Woolnoth after [T. C.] Wageman.
f.17v	Michael Balfe, photograph.
f.18	J. L. Hatton, photograph.
f.18	J. K. Pyne, photograph.
f.20	Sir George Macfarren, after a photograph by Elliott & Fry.
f.21	William Macfarren, photograph.
f.31	Sir William Sterndale Bennett, lithograph by Baugniet. 1844.
f.31v	Sir Julius Benedict; Mary Benedict, lithographs.
f.32	Sir Julius Benedict, lithograph by Baugniet. 1844.
f.36	Vincent Novello, engraving.
f.37	Louis George Jullien, engraving.

f.37	D. F. E. Auber, lithograph by L. Billiard (?) after (?).
f.37v	D. F. E. Auber, photograph.
f.37v	Offenbach, photograph.
f.38	J. S. Bach, engraving, including scenes of Leipzig, by A. H. Payne after H. Bibby.
f.38-42	Handel, various engravings.
f.42v	Gluck, engraving.
f.44-45	Mozart, various engravings and photographs of paintings, some not authentic.
f.46-47	Beethoven, various engravings and photographs of paintings, some not authentic.
f.47v	Weber, engravings by A. H. Payne.
f.48v	B. Molique, engraving.
f.49	P. Lindpaintner, engraving by Carl Mayer.
f.51	Ignaz Moscheles, lithograph by Baugniet. 1846.
f.55	Mendelssohn, various engravings.
f.57	Spohr, lithograph by M. Gauci.
f.58	Spohr, lithograph by W. Pfaff. [Before 1822.].
f.59	Franz Cramer, engraving.
f.60	J. B. Cramer, lithograph by W. Sharp. 1830.
f.61	Joseph Mainzer, engraving.
f.61v	J. Woelfl, water-colour drawing.
f.62	Johann Strauss, the elder, lithograph by Kriehuber. 1835.
f.62	S. Heller, photograph by Walery, Paris.
f.63	J. N. Hummel, lithograph by W. Sharp.
f.64,65v	Robert Schumann, photographs.
f.66	Wagner, engraving, and photograph.
f.66v	Meyerbeer, photograph.
f.68	Meyerbeer, engraving.
f.69	Clementi, engraving.
f.76	Donizetti, photograph of a drawing (?).
f.71	Rossini, engraving by R. Morgen after E. Cateni. 1822; and photograph.
f.72	Verdi, photograph of a painting (?).
f.73	Sir Michael Costa, engraving.
f.74	Sir John Stainer, chromolithograph by 'Spy'.
f.75	A. Dreyschock, lithograph. 1843.
f.75v	Mrs. Lucy Anderson, lithograph.

f.76	S. Thalberg, lithograph by Kriehuber. 1838.
f.77	Clara Schumann, photograph.
f.78b	Liszt, photograph by Ganz, Brussels.
f.79	A reception given for Liszt at Grosvenor House, London, 8 April 1886. The group includes Sullivan, W. Shakespeare, Joachim, Arthur Chappell, Antoinette Sterling, Sir George Macfarren, Otto Goldschmidt, Sir August Manns, Walter Bache, Sir Charles Hallé, Madame Albani. Woodcut.
f.79v	Sir Charles Hallé, photograph.
f.80	Anton Rubenstein, lithograph.
f.81	Ernst Pauer, lithograph by Baugniet. 1851.
f.81v	Joseph Hofmann as a child, from a photograph by Elliott & Fry.
f.82	'Master Mori' (Nicolo Mori), engraving. [1805?].
f.83	Ole Bull, lithograph.
f.84	Paganini, lithograph by W. Sharp after Maurin. 1831.
f.85	Camillo Sivori, lithograph by Kriebuber. 1841.
f.86	H. W. Ernst, lithograph by M. & N. Hanhart.
f.87	Joachim, photograph by Elliott & Fry.
f.88	Dragonetti, engraving.
f.90	Thomas Harper, lithograph by H. Barraud.
f.90v	Pasta, lithograph by M. Gauci.
f.91	Catalani, lithograph; Mary Ann Paton, lithograph; Pasta, engraving by T. Woolnoth after Dubase; Miss Stephens (Countess of Essex), engraving; Sonntag, engraving.
f.92	Malibran, lithograph by Minasi after a medal by Vitt. Nesti. 1836; Malibran as Fidelio, lithograph by W. Sharp after W. H. Wontner.
f.93	Adelaide Kemble as Norma, lithograph.
f.93v	Clara Novello, engraving; Anna Bishop, photograph.
f.97	Grisi, engraving.
f.99	Louisa Bodda Pyne, photograph.
f.101	Fanny Persiani as Rosina, engraving.
f.102,103	Jenny Lind, engravings.

f.103	Albert Smith and John Orlando Parry, woodcuts.
f.104	John Orlando Parry, lithograph by Baugniet. 1845.
f.106	G. B. Rubini, lithograph by Kriehuber.
f.109	Joseph Staudigl, lithograph by J. Bekel.
f.110	Henry Phillips, lithograph by Baugniet. 1846.
f.111	John Braham, engraving by Thomson after [Thomas] Foster; engraving by [? E. J.] Roberts.
f.113	Sims Reeves, engraving.
36747	
f.70	Gounod, photograph by Ch. Reutliger.
f.71	Gounod, engraving by W. Krauskopf.
f.72	Gounod, engraving by L. M.
f.73	Gounod, engraving by A. Masson after the bust by J. B. Carpeaux.
f.74	Gounod, lithograph. 1893.
f.75	William Vincent Wallace, photograph.
38072	
f.1	Christophorus Hitzenauer, engraving.
f.2	Johannes Andreas Herbst, engraving by H. Ammon after Sebastian Furck. 1635.
f.3	William Inglott, engraving. [c.1625].
f.4	J. S. Bach, engraving by E. Griessmann.
f.5	J. S. Bach, engraving by S. G. Kütner after G. Haussmann. 1774.
f.6	J. S. Bach, engraving by L. Sichling after G. Haussmann.
f.7	C. F. Hurlebosch, mezzotint, proof before all letters, by P. A. Wakkerdak after Oswald Wynen.
f.8	Handel, engraving by F. Bartolozzi after G. B. Cipriani.
f.9	Handel, engraving by F. C. Lewis after Francis Kite. 1828.
f.10	Handel, apotheosis, engraving by James Heath after Biagio Rebecca. 1787.
f.11	'Concerto spirituale'. A caricature, etching by James Betterton (after H. W. Bunbury). 1773.

A group of three musicians playing viol da gamba, horn and oboe.

f.12 'Concerto spirituale'. The same caricature as f.11, (re-etched by a different hand) after H. W. Bunbury, on later paper and on a smaller scale. A pencil note names the players as 'Bach', 'Ponto', 'Fisher'. Of these, the first seems very doubtful; the gamba player is more likely to be C. F. Abel. 'Ponto' may be a corruption of the surname of Giovanni Punto, the famous Bohemian hornist, born Jan Stich. 'Fisher' is almost certainly the well-known oboist Johann Christian Fischer.

f.13 C. P. E. Bach, engraving.

f.14 C. P. E. Bach, silhouette.

f.15 C. P. E. Bach, engraving.

f.16 C. P. E. Bach, engraving by A. Stöttrup.

f.17 J. C. Bach, monument, 1783, engraving by Bartolozzi after Aug. [Agostino] Carlini. 1791.

f.18 Mozart, engraving by Johann Neidl after a plaster medallion by Leonard Posch. [1800.].

f.19 Mendelssohn, lithograph by R. J. Hamerton after Kelser. 1834.

f.20 Robert Schumann, engraving by Auguste Hüssener.

49350B

ff.13,14 photographs by Alfred Ellis, London, of a production of Gilbert and Sullivan's *Trial by Jury*, including Lytton as the judge.

49351A

Fourteen photographs by Alfred Ellis, London, of a performance of Gilbert and Sullivan's *The Sorcerer*, 17 November 1898.

Eleven photographs by Alfred Ellis & Wallery, London, of a performance of Gilbert and Sullivan's *HMS Pinafore*, 1899, including Lytton as Captain Corcoran.

49351B

Eleven photographs by Barraud, London, of a performance of Gilbert and Sullivan's *Ruddigore.*

49351C

Fifty-six photographs by Alfred Ellis, London, of a performance of Gilbert and Sullivan's *Utopia Limited*, including Rutland Barrington as King Paramount.

50238

Photographs of William Baines; one photograph of Moiseivitch.

50813-15

Photographs of Ernö Dohnányi, at all periods of his life from about aged 20 to 1960.

51066

Photographs of Ernö Dohnányi, mostly in his maturity.

56443A

A collection of photographs, mostly of or relating to Sir Henry J. Wood. It includes some thirty of Wood, from the age of 3 (1872) to 74 (1943), either by himself or with others, eg Sir Adrian Boult and Vaughan Williams. Among the photographs of Wood conducting is one showing the Queen's Hall in 1934. A group of four Russian photographs shows a gathering of the All-Union Society for Cultural Relations (VOKS), which sent congratulations to Wood on his seventy-fifth birthday in March 1944. Among the musicians are Prokofiev, Glier, Aleksandrov, and Viktor Belyayev. There is also a photograph of Shostakovich in 1943 (?). A group photograph of musicians in Hollywood (1942?) shows John and Evelyn Barbirolli, Alfred Kastner, Henri de Busscher, and Emile Ferir. A photograph of an Albert Hall concert shows Bruno Walter conducting Mahler's second symphony, with Kathleen Ferrier and Dora van Doorn as soloists.

57845

Two photographs of Vaughan Williams, by Karsh of Ottawa, 1949.

Portraits of musicians are found in the following Egerton manuscript:

3097B

f.15-18 Felix, Rebecca, Fanny and Paul Mendelssohn as children. Photographs, by Loetscher & Petsch, Berlin, of paintings.

f.21 Paul Mendelssohn, photograph by F. Jamrath, Berlin. [1871?].

f.27 S. S. Wesley, photograph by Aug. F. Perren, Bath.

f.28 Eliza Wesley, photograph by Fred. T. Palmer, St. Lawrence on Sea.

f.31 Verdi, photograph by P. Tempestini, Viareggio. Signed by Verdi 1901.

f.35 Sir William Sterndale Bennett, photograph of a painting.

f.38 Sir George Elvey, photograph by Elliott & Fry.

f.39 Felix Moscheles, photograph. Signed by Moscheles 1913.

Portraits of musicians are found in the Royal Philharmonic Society's collection.

Loan 48. 15/4

George Frederick Anderson, Joseph Williams, J. McMurdie, Frederick Bowen Jewson, J. T. Calkin, directors of the society, with Stanley Lucas (secretary) and William George Cusins (conductor), grouped round the bust of Beethoven by Franz Schaller. Photograph taken 20 May 1871 by the London Stereoscopic & Photographic Company, at their premises where the directors held this special meeting.

Loan 48. 15/5

f.5 Gerhard von Breuning. Photograph, headed in manuscript 'Beethoven's Ariel 1857 Wien', by F. K. Strezek, Vienna.

f.6 Karl Holz. Photograph, dated in manuscript '4 5 58'.

f.7 Paul Friedrich Walther. Photograph, dated in manuscript '18 9 60'.

f.8 Fanny Linzbauer. Photograph by Doctor es Kozmata, Pest.

f.9 Willem Mengelberg. Caricature by Barton Wilkinson.

f.10 Charles Neate. Photograph by H. Lenthall, London.

f.10 Euphrosyne Parepa-Rosa. Two photographs, by the London Stereoscopic & Photographic

Company, (a) at the harmonium (b) half-length, dated in manuscript 'July 1872'.

f.11 Wassily Safonoff. Photograph by Falk, New York.

f.14 Helen Lemmens-Sherrington. Two different photographs by R. W. Thrupp, Birmingham, both signed by the singer.

Instruments

There are numerous drawings, many accompanied by descriptions, of about 100 different types of instruments, many with players, and including groups of instruments, in the manuscripts of the Department. They range from the Middle Ages up to the nineteenth century. A selected list of them, with references, is included in vol.III of the Hughes-Hughes catalogue (see p.62 above). A manuscript of this type, not included in Hughes-Hughes's list, is Stowe 1081:

A manuscript of French songs on vellum, late seventeenth century, including drawings of performers.

f.1v a female lutenist.

f.22 a female dancer, with castanets.

f.24r a masked male dancer, playing a long-necked, four-stringed instrument.

f.29v two male singers.

f.31v,32r nine dancers, male and female.

The material relating to the history of instruments also includes:

17480

The journal of Thomas Dallam, organ builder, relating his voyage from London to Constantinople and back, 1599-1600, undertaken to convey to the Sultan of Turkey, as a present from Elizabeth I, the organ which he had constructed. F.55v describes the instrument in some detail.

33965

f.168 A description by J. S. Bach, in his autograph, 1746, of an organ at Zschortau, made by Johann Scheibe of Leipzig.

39861

'The construction of flutes and their last improvements', by Theobald Boehm, in his autograph. Before 1882.

41636-9

Correspondence of Alfred Hipkins, and some members of his family, with English and foreign specialists, concerning early instruments.

49633-7

Collections made by J. Leslie Stephen, relating to the history of the piano. They include: records of travel, undertaken in 1920 and 1921, to amass facts about export markets; notes and drawings about construction, 1903-18; historical notes on pianos. (For the printed portion of Stephen's collection, see pp.56-7 supra.)

Letters

The quantity of letters written by musicians is considerable. In any period, they form the stuff of musical history. To give but one instance, from the twentieth century, the collections of Edward Clark and Sir Adrian Boult record some of the part played by the BBC in English musical life. The letters may be divided for convenience into three categories:

(i) Single letters, or a small group of letters by one writer, or by similar writers.

(ii) A group of letters, by various writers, amassed by a collector who, in most cases, was not the recipient.

(iii) A large group of letters collected either by a single recipient, whether an individual or an institution, or by two or more recipients in the same family.

In category (i) there are no examples extant before the later part of the sixteenth century, and the earliest letters are in the nature of petitions usually relating to matters of payment of salary. Such are those by a number of Italian musicians active at the English court – Alfonso Ferrabosco I and Pietro and Gioseffo Lupo – in Cotton Titus B vii. ff.48, 131, 156, 231, 309, 331, 344, and 358, mostly addressed to the Earl of Sussex. Similar letters in Cotton Titus B ii are written by the 'brothers Bassano' (here without Christian names) on behalf of their brother Eduardo (f.215), and by

Gioseffo Lupo (f.205). Matters of salary payments run on well into the seventeenth century, and are found in letters written by or relating to John, Clement and Andrea Lanier in 1645 and 1649 (Egerton 2159, ff.6,8-10). Of a rather more personal character is a letter (46378B, f.11) written in Italian by Angelo Notari in 1642 and addressed from Grange – a hamlet in the West of England – to Dr. Samuel Bave in Bath, asking primarily for a medical prescription.

The collections include a representation of letters by eighteenth century composers, among them two of the few still extant written by Handel – one, of 1716 (33965, f.204), addressed to an official of the South Sea Company, the other, of 24 February 1750 (24182, f.15), relating to the hire of an artillery kettle-drum for use in his oratorios. There is a group written by Mozart to his cousin Maria Anna Thekla Mozart, in the Stefan Zweig collection, already mentioned (Loan 42: see p.76). There is a fine letter (48590K) written by Gluck in 1778 to his close friend and regular correspondent Franz Kruthoffer. The holding of Beethoven's letters is fully listed in *Beethoven and England*, by Pamela Willetts (see p.44). From the romantic period are three letters by Meyerbeer, a dozen by Wagner, a group of ten by Berlioz (56237), and one by Max Bruch. It is not really until the turn of the century that letters by European composers are found regularly in the collections, and then generally as a result of their correspondence with English musicians.

In category (ii) the three principal collections are:

33965

Formed by Andrew George Kurtz, secretary of the Liverpool Philharmonic Society. The collection includes letters by T. A. Arne, J. S. Bach, Bellini, Berlioz, Boyce, Donizetti, Orlando Gibbons, Handel, F. J. Haydn, Henry Lawes, Lind, Lock, Mendelssohn, Rossini, Schumann, Harriet Smithson, Verdi, Weber.

38071

Formed by Alfred Morten, includes letters by Gounod, F. J. Haydn, Hummel, Mercadante, Pacini, Spohr, Clara Schumann, Robert Schumann, Spontini, Sullivan.

41628

Formed by Johann Ernst Perabo (1845-1920), a German

musician who ultimately settled in the United States. The collection includes letters by Beethoven, Berlioz, Brahms, Czerny, Ferdinand David, Robert Franz, N. W. Gade, Liszt, Mendelssohn, Leopold Mozart, W. A. Mozart, Clara Schumann, Robert Schumann, Spontini, Weber.

The following collections, which form category (iii), are arranged in numerical order, those in the Additional series being followed by five groups in other series and one group on loan. The name of the recipient stands after the number, and the approximate dates of the collection as a whole are given in brackets at the end. In most cases only a selection of the writers is named.

11730
Vincent Novello, from Thomas Adams, Attwood, Burney, Crotch, C. F. Horn, Charles Lamb, Latrobe, Mendelssohn, I. Moscheles, William Russell, Shield. (1810-40)

17838
Domenico Dragonetti, from Thomas Alsager, Lucy Anderson, Sir Henry Bishop, Bochsa, N. Mori, V. Novello, C. Potter, G. H. Rodwell, M. Schlesinger, Sir George Smart, W. Watts, Yaniewicz. (c.1796-1846)

35263-65
George Thomson, from Beethoven, Bishop, Haydn, Hummel, Koželuch, Weber. All the letters relate to accompaniments supplied for Thomson's collections of national song. Some of the letters by Beethoven and Haydn are written by an amanuensis and signed by the composer. (1797-1847)

39679
William Barclay Squire, from Sir George Grove. (1878-98)

39680
William Barclay Squire, from Sir W. G. Cusins, Edward Dannreuther, Robert Eitner, Edmund Gurney, Franz Haberl, Sir Augustus Harris, Henry James, Sir August Manns, Alfredo Piatti, Sir George Scharf, Sir John Stainer, Charles Edward Stephens, J. Addington Symonds. (1879-1909)

42233
Edward Speyer, from Frank Bridge, Grove, Hadow,

Henschel, Parry, A. Piatti, William Shakespeare, Stanford, Goring Thomas. (1876-1930)

42718

Joachim, family, from Joseph Joachim to his parents Julius and Fanny Joachim and to his brother Friedrich, with some letters from his wife Amalie (née Weiss). (1839-81)

47216

Augustus Hughes-Hughes, from W. F. H. Blandford, Charles van den Borren, William Chappell, W. H. Cummings, W. Warde Fowler, Frank Kidson, W. Westley Manning, J. Kendrick Pyne, Count G. de Saint-Foix, T. L. Southgate. (1883-1922)

47602

Theodore Ritter, Sir Charles Hallé, etc. from Hector Berlioz. (1848-60)

50360

Ralph Vaughan Williams, from Maurice Ravel. (1908-19)

50529

George Bernard Shaw, from Rutland Boughton. (1912-45)

50852

William Barclay Squire, from G. E. P. Arkwright, Edwin Ashdown, Frank Kidson, Sir George Scharf, O. G. Sonneck. (c.1890-1908)

52256-7

Edward Clark, from Bartok, Bax, Berg, Britten, Dallapiccola, Delius, Dent, Heseltine, Hindemith, Schönberg, Stravinsky, Tippett, Vaughan Williams, Walton, Webern, Sir H. Wood. (1921-52)

52364

Rutland Boughton, from Bantock, Bax, Beecham, Dent, Elgar, Ferrier, Holst, Paul Robeson. (1913-55)

52365

Rutland Boughton, from George Bernard Shaw. (1908-50)

52547

Philip Heseltine, from Frederick Delius (in his hand up to 1922, dictated by him to Jelka Delius, 1923-30). (1911-30)

53767

Benno Hollander, from Saint-Saens. (1892-1915?)

53768
Benno Hollander, from Beecham, Boult, Busoni, Paul Hirsch, Pitt, Stanford. (c.1904-c.1930)
56361
Rosamond Ley, from F. Busoni and Gerda Busoni, with letters from F. Busoni to Miss Mary Bruce. (1909-56)
56426
Sir Henry Wood, from Dimitri Shostakovich. (1942-44)
56428-30
Sir Henry Wood and Lady Jessie Wood, from Boughton, Boult, Britten, Clara Butt, Casals, Jelka Delius, Ferrier, L. Goosens, Grainger, A. Gretchaninov, Malipiero, Elizabeth Schumann, G. Bernard Shaw, Stokowski, Stravinsky, Sullivan, Szigeti, Weingartner. (1898-c.1945)
57784
Cecil Gray, from Delius, G. B. Shaw, Sibelius. (1916-c.1950)
57838-40
Estelle and Stuart Fletcher, daughter and son-in-law of Rutland Boughton, from Rutland Boughton. (1928-60)
60498-9
Sir Adrian Boult, from N. Boulanger, Casals, W. Damrosch, Delius, Elgar, Kodaly, Sibelius, Vaughan Williams, Bruno Walter. (1907-78)
Egerton 3158
Professor Carl Mayreder and Frau Rosa Mayreder (librettist of *Der Corregidor*), from Hugo Wolf. (1895-8)
Egerton 3301-2
Percy Pitt, from Hans Richter, and some letters to Richter from Pitt. (1903-13)
Egerton 3303
Percy Pitt, from Elgar, and some letters to Elgar from Pitt. F.56 is a printed rehearsal schedule for the Gloucester Music Festival, September 1928. (1899-1932)
Egerton 3304-6
Percy Pitt, from Albanesi, Ansermet, Harold Bauer, Boughton, Delius, Destinn, N. Gatty, A. Genée, Sir E. German, L. Godowsky, Robert Heger, Holst, Koussevitsky, Kreisler, Lamond, I. de Lara, Mengelberg, Monteux, Nikisch, Horatio Parker, Puccini, E. de Reszke, Rhein-

berger, Ropartz, Saint-Saens, Franz Schalk, Richard Strauss, C. S. Terry, Maggie Teyte, Tosti, Siegfried Wagner, Weingartner, Wolf-Ferrari, Ysaÿe, Zandonai. (1892-1932)

Sloane 1388, ff.56-108

Rev. William Holder, mostly from John Baynard, with others from John Carr and John Heptinstall, relating to the printing of Holder's *Treatise on the natural Grounds and Principles of Harmony*. (1692-4)

Loan 48/13

The Philharmonic (after 1914, Royal Philharmonic) Society, some 6,000 letters, principally from composers, conductors, soloists and members of the Society. Bound in alphabetical order in 38 volumes. There is also a volume of letters written on behalf of sovereigns of England, who range from George IV (as Prince Regent) to Elizabeth II, and on behalf of other members of the royal family. The musicians include Beecham, Beethoven, Berlioz, Brahms, Britten, Debussy, Delius, Dvořák, Elgar, Grieg, Holst, Kreisler, Liszt, Lutosławski, Pachmann, Rachmaninov, Shostakovich, Sibelius, Spohr, Richard Strauss, Tchaikovsky, Vaughan Williams, Wagner. (1813-1976)

Libretti

The following are among Additional manuscripts containing libretti:

27831

ff.272-86 *The Prisoner's Opera* [by Edward Ward]: *to which is added, several other entertainments perform'd at Sadler's Wells.* London, 1727. The printed libretto, with the music. pp.20.7. Ff.254-6 give an account of the performance.

38622

ff.1-52 An English version of Weber's opera *Der Freischütz*, by W. McGregor Logan. 1824.

ff.69-163 *The Incas or the Peruvian virgin*, by John Thelwell. First produced 1792.

ff.165-87 The words of the songs of *Harlequin Omai*, by John O'Keefe. 1785.

37968

La donna di genio volubile, music by Marcos Antonio Portugal (Portogallo), text by Giuseppe Bertati. c.1800.

47220

Sisyphus, opera by Baron Bodog Orczy. With printed libretto by Frederick and H. L. Corder. 1884.

47688

The Ring and the Keeper, operetta, music by W. H. Montgomery, libretto by John Pratt Wooler. c.1859.

47895

The Pilgrim's Progress, symphonic drama, intended to be set to music by Elgar. Typescript libretto by Richard Alexander Streatfeild, followed by a manuscript of three leaves in his hand, the first leaf headed 'Prologue (suggested)', the second and third containing an outline of the musical action. Before 1914.

50170

The Maid of the Mountains, musical play by Harold Fraser-Simson. Typescript libretto. c.1917.

50171

A Southern Maid, musical play, by Harold Fraser-Simson. Typescript libretto. c.1917.

50172

The Street Singer, musical play by Harold Fraser-Simson. Typescript libretto. c.1924.

50272

Consists entirely of libretti for operas by Giulio Cottrau and of scripts based on these libretti, as follows:

Printed:

1 *Griselda. Dramma lirico in tre atti da Enrico Goliscani.* Siena. 1893.

2 *Griseldis. Lyrisches Drama . . . Deutsch von Ludwig Hartmann.* Sondershausen. 1893.

3 *Griselda.* [Rome, 1902].

4 *La lege lombarda.* Roma, 1907.

5 *Cordelia.* Padova, 1913.

6 *Pericle, rè di Tiro.* Roma, n.d.

7 *Giovanna d'Arco.* Rome, 1924.

8 *Griselda.* n.d., n.p.

9 *Griselda.* Riassunto del libretto e motivi principale della musica. [1891].

MS or typescript:

10,11 Disposizone scenica per l'opera Griselda.

12,13 *Cordelia.* Cinedramma.

14 *Pericle rè di Tiro.*

15 *Joan of Arc.* Musical poem.

54210

Where the Rainbow ends, musical play, by Roger Quilter. Typescript libretto. c.1911.

Programmes

The following Additional manuscripts contain programmes:

29804

ff.26,27 Rough draft, in Paganini's autograph, of the programme of a concert given by him in Vienna 26 May 1828, with the printed programme.

32238

(all printed at Weimar)

f.1-9 *Concert zur Feyer des zweyten Februars.* 1821. 1823.

f.10 *Programm. Musikalischer Abend.* 1827.

f.11-21 *Festcantate zum zweyten Februar.* 1827. 1828.

f.35-38 *Festcantate.* 18 May 1823.

33507

f.242 A printed programme, *Programme de la grande fête musicale à Cologne . . . 7 et 8 juin 1835 sous la direction de Mr. Felix Mendelssohn Bartholdy . . . grande salle de Gurzenich.*

33965

ff.265,398 Draft programmes in Mendelssohn's hand for concerts at the Leipzig Gewandhaus, 1 January to 23 March 1843.

35017

A record of concerts given by Charles Wesley (b.1757) and Samuel Wesley (b.1766) in 1779 to 1785 at their

London home: with lists of subscribers and others, the names of those present, and accounts. A copy, made from the original by Eliza Wesley.

35027

f.3v Two printed programmes of organ recitals given by Thomas Adams, 8 November 1850 and 4 March 1832, at Gray & Davison's organ manufactory, 9 New Road, Fitzroy Square, London.

f.54 Three printed programmes of Mendelssohn's *St. Paul*, performed by the Sacred Harmonic Society, Exeter Hall, 28 June 1844, 2 June 1845, 30 April 1847, the first and third conducted by the composer.

38071

f.43 A printed programme, *Dinner given by the musical Profession to Mr. J. B. Cramer before his Departure from England, Freemason's Tavern, July 15, 1835.*

41775

A collection of printed programmes (bills of performance) made by Sir George Smart during his European tour, July to December 1825. The programmes relate mainly to opera, in the following cities – Brussels, Frankfurt, Darmstadt, Stuttgart, Munich, Linz, Vienna, Prague, Dresden, Leipzig, Hanover, Cassel, Cologne, Brussels.

49603

Printed programmes of the concerts of the Musical League given at Liverpool, September 1909.

51067

Printed programmes of concerts at which Ernö Dohnányi appeared, either as pianist or conductor, in the following places, from 1904 to 1928: Amsterdam, Baltimore, Bergen, Bologna, Budapest, Boston (Mass.), Brunn, Genoa, Harrogate, London, Manchester, Marburg, New York, Oxford, Randers (Holland), Salzburg, San Francisco, Stockholm, Trieste, Yale (New Haven), Zagreb.

60379

Printed programme of the Birmingham Festival, 25 September 1840 comprising 'portion of the oratorio of

Jeptha' abridged by William Ayrton. With printed lists of the chorus and orchestra. There is also a printed copy of the *Commemoration of Handel*, 1784, with MS list of receipts and payments.

Miscellanea

The collections contain much biographical and historical material. While the greater part is British, there are also documents relating to foreign music. The following gives a few examples of both.

For the earlier periods, a good deal consists of a leaf or a few leaves in a miscellaneous volume of manuscripts. These documents are in the nature of brief notices, grants or payments, made by royal, civic, or ecclesiastical authority. There are also accounts, lists of establishments, and the like. Other manuscripts are very diverse in character. From such a numerous field, only a few examples can be given. A register of the Abbey of Bury St. Edmund's (Harley 645), made in the mid-fifteenth century, includes (ff.86,86v) copies of letters written by various ecclesiastics against the establishment of private singing schools in the town. Two manuscripts of the later eighteenth century (15003, ff.93v-98v, and 15022, ff.113-117) give an account copied from early sources of an Eisteddfod held at Caermarthen by Griffith ap Nicholas, who died in 1461. In Lansdowne 171 (ff.249,249v and f.252v) are notes, made from a royal establishment book, of payments to musicians in the reign of Edward IV. There is a warrant of Elizabeth I, dated 26 April 1585, permitting Thomas Gyles, master of St. Paul's choir school, to find children suitable for training in his school (Sloane 2035B, f.2). Sloane 2329 comprises the Gresham lectures on the history of music delivered in February 1610 by John Taverner, a doctor in medicine, who was the second Gresham Professor, in succession to John Bull. Seven of the nine lectures are in Latin, two, contrary to the statutes, in English. Among the Hardwicke Papers is the list of the state band at Dublin Castle in 1801 (27686, ff.3-12).

Foreign documents are equally various, though less numerous. There are, for example, a record of Calvin's attitude to church music (Sloane 1021, f.15); a list of mid-seventeenth century churches, monasteries and the like in Naples, which housed thirty-six conservatories for women and children (20924, ff.176-197v); and receipts for salaries from two 'Surintendantes de la musique de la chambre du Roy', of 1633, and 1634 (Egerton 2159, f.4,5). One of the most notable English eighteenth century manuscripts is the journal (35122) kept by Charles Burney of the tour that he made from June to December 1770 through France and Italy. This journal was later published as *The Present State of Music in France and Italy*. A view of musical history and aesthetics from a rather later generation is found in the lectures (35014-15) given mostly in London and Bristol by Samuel Wesley, at various dates from 1811 to 1830.

Sundry manuscripts cover some peripheral aspects of music. One such is 'A description of all the musical birds in this Kingdom' by John Hammersley (29892, early eighteenth century), which includes a method of teaching them to whistle, and songbird tunes. Quite a numerous group contributes to the history of English campanology over three and a half centuries. They range from instructions for bell-ringing at Westminster in 1504 (Harley 1498, ff.13, 14v, 21, 28v), to the ringing of Bow bells in the 1680s (29283, f.3), and various lists of change-ringing, and descriptions, both manuscript and printed, of bells, singers and the like, throughout England in the eighteenth and nineteenth centuries, in the collections made by E. J. Osborn (19370, 19368-9). This section is the appropriate place to mention the autograph of *Catechism of Instrumentation*, an unpublished book by John Hiles, the author of several successful printed works in this form. As an example of orchestral writing for the harp, Hiles (d.1882) cites Bruch's little known choral piece *Odysseus*, 1872.

Literature

Backhouse, Janet M., 'Delius Letters [Add. MSS 52547-9]' *British Museum Quarterly*, XXX, 1965, 30-33.

Bent, Margaret, 'Initial Letters in the Old Hall Manuscript,' *Music & Letters*, 47, 1966, 225-38.

Bent, Margaret, 'The Old Hall Manuscript [Add. MS 57950]', *Early Music*, 2, 1974, 2-14.

Blezzard, Judith, 'The Lumley Books. A collection of Tudor church music [Royal Appendix 74-76]', *Musical Times*, 112, 1971, 128-30.

Blezzard, Judith, 'A new Source of Tudor secular Music. [Add. MS 60577]', *Musical Times*, 122, 1981, 532-5.

Bray, Roger W., 'British Museum Add. MSS 17802-5. (The Gyffard part books: an index and commentary)', *Royal Musical Association Research Chronicle*, 7, 1969, 31-50.

Bukofzer, Manfred, *"Sumer is icumen in" A revision.* [Harley 978.] Berkeley & Los Angeles, 1944. (University of California Publications in Music. vol.2, no.2).

Burney, Charles, *Men, Music and Manners in France and Italy 1770. Being the journal written by Charles Burney during a tour through those countries undertaken to collect material for 'A General History of Music'. Transcribed from the original manuscript in the British Museum, Additional Manuscript 35122, and edited with an introduction by H. Edmund Poole.* pp.xxix.245. Folio Society: London, 1969.

Cadell, Patrick M., ' 'Patience' and 'The Gondoliers' (Add. MSS 53777-9. The autograph scores)', *British Museum Quarterly*, XXXII, 1968, 4-6.

Chan, Mary, 'John Hilton's manuscript British Library Add. MS 11608', *Music & Letters*, 60, 1979, 440-9.

Cobbe, Hugh, 'British musical Autographs' [on an exhibition of recent acquisitions], *Musical Times*, 114, 1973, 793-4.

Cobbe, Hugh, 'Papers of Sir Henry Wood [Add. MSS 56419-43]', *British Museum Quarterly*, XXXVI, 1971, 11-15.

Cyr, Mary, 'A seventeenth-century Source of Ornamentation for Voice and Viol: British Museum MS. Egerton 2971', *Royal Musical Association Research Chronicle*, 9, 1971, 53-72.

Dart, Thurston, 'Robert ap Huw's Manuscript of Welsh harp Music (ca.1613) [Add. MS 14905]', *Galpin Society Journal*, XXI, 1968, 52-65.

Emery, Walter, 'The London autograph of "The Forty-Eight" [Add. MS 35021]', *Music & Letters*, 34, 1953, 106-123.

Field, Christopher D. S., 'Musical Observations from Barbados. [Add. MS 23779]', *Musical Times*, 115, 1974, 565-67.

Gillingham, Brian, 'British Library MS Egerton 945: further evidence for the mensural interpretation of sequences', *Music & Letters*, 61, 1980, 50-9.

Gransden, K. W., and Willetts, Pamela, 'Papers of W. S. Gilbert [Add. MSS 48289-353 and 49289-306]', *British Museum Quarterly*, XXI, 1958, 67-9.

Hadden, J. C., *George Thomson. His life and correspondence.* J. A. Nimmo: London, 1898. Pp.293-335, 'Correspondence about the music', are based on Add. MSS 35263-9, which relate to the accompaniments supplied to Thomson by Koželuch, Haydn, Beethoven, Bishop, Weber and Hummel, for his editions of Scottish, Welsh and Irish songs.

Handschin, Jacques, 'The Summer Canon and its Background [Harley MS 978]', *Musica Disciplina*, III, 1949, 74-94.

Hughes, Andrew, and Bent, Margaret, 'The Old Hall Manuscript [Add. MS 57950]. A reappraisal by A. Hughes, and inventory, by A. Hughes and M. Bent', *Musica Disciplina*, XXI, 1967, 97-147.

Joiner, Mary, 'British Museum Add. MS 15117. An index, commentary and bibliography', *Royal Musical Association Research Chronicle*, 7, 1969, 51-109; 8, 1970, 102.

Kerman, Joseph, 'Beethoven Sketchbooks in the British Museum', *Proceedings of the Royal Musical Association*, 93, 1966-67, 77-96.

King, A. H., 'Haydn's Trio for Horn, Violin and Cello. [Hob.IV 5*: Add. MS 46172. A copy, made from the now lost autograph by E. Mandyczewski]', *Musical Times*, 86, 1945, 367.

Knowlton, Jean, 'Dating the Masque dramas in the British Museum, Additional MS. 10444', *British Musical Quarterly*, XXXII, 1968, 99-102.

Leeson, Daniel N., and Whitwell, David, 'Mozart's thematic Catalogue [Loan 42.1]', *Musical Times*, 104, 1973, 781-3.

Mayes, Stanley, *An Organ for the Sultan*, Putnam: London, 1956. [On the instrument made by Thomas Dallam, and his journey with it to Constantinople, 1599-1600, as described in Add. 17480.].

Maynard, Judson D., 'Heir beginnis countering [Add. MS

4911]', *Journal of the American Musicological Society*, XX, 1967, 182-196.

Monson, Craig, 'Thomas Myriell's Manuscript Collection: one view of musical taste in Jacobean London [chiefly on Add. MSS 29372-7]', *Journal of the American Musicological Society*, XXX, 1977, 419-65.

Neighbour, O. W., 'New Consort Music by Byrd [Egerton MS 3307]', *Musical Times*, 108, 1967, 506-08.

Noiray, Michel, and Parker, Roger, 'La composition d'Attila [by Verdi], étude de quelques variantes [chiefly on the complete autograph Add. MS 35156 and the sketch of the prologue Paris BN MS 2208]', *Revue de musicologie*, 62, 1976, 104-24.

Oldman, Cecil B., 'J. A. André on Mozart's Manuscripts [Add. MS 32412]', *Music & Letters*, 5, 1924, 169-76.

Polin, Claire, 'Observations on the Ap Huw Manuscript [Add MS 14905]', *Music & Letters*, 60, 1980, 296-304.

Poole, H. Edmund, 'Music engraving Practice in eighteenth-century London: a study of some Forster editions of Haydn and their manuscript sources [Egerton MSS 2379 and 2335]', *Music and Bibliography*. Edited by O. W. Neighbour, Saur/Bingley: London, New York, 1980, 98-131.

Poole, H. Edmund, 'The Printing of Holder's 'Principles of Harmony' [with special reference to Sloane MS 1388 ff.56-108b]', *Proceedings of the Royal Musical Association*, 101, 1975, 31-44.

Sandon, Nick, 'Mary, Meditations, Monks and Music. Poetry, prose, processions and plagues in a Durham Cathedral manuscript [Royal MS 7. A.VI]', *Early Music*, 10, 1982, 43-55.

Schofield, Bertram, 'The Autograph Manuscript of Stanford's Revenge', *British Museum Quarterly*, III, 1929, 77.

Schofield, Bertram, 'The Adventures of an English Minstrel and his Varlet [Egerton MS 3509]', *Musical Quarterly*, 35, 1949, 361-76.

Schofield, Bertram, 'An Autograph of Borodin [Egerton MS 3087]', *British Museum Quarterly*, VIII, 1933, 31-2.

Schofield, Bertram, 'An early Dvořák MS. [Add. MS 42050.

The cello concerto in A major]', *British Museum Quarterly*, V, 1930, 25-6.

Schofield, Bertram, 'Early Italian Songs [Egerton MS 3051]', *British Museum Quarterly*, VI, 1932, 51-2.

Schofield, Bertram, 'Elgar's unfinished Symphony [Add. MS 56101]', *British Museum Quarterly*, X, 1936, 112-3.

Schofield, Bertram, 'Letters of Joseph Joachim [Add. MS 42718]', *British Museum Quarterly*, VII, 1933, 22-3.

Schofield, Bertram, 'The Manuscripts of Tallis's forty-part Motet. [Egerton MS 3512 and other MSS]', *Musical Quarterly*, XXXVII, 1951, 176-183.

Schofield, Bertram, 'A newly discovered 15th-century Manuscript of the English Chapel Royal [the *Windsor Carol Book*, Egerton MS 3307]', – Part 1. *Musical Quarterly*, XXXII, 1946, 509-36.

Schofield, Bertram, 'Papers of the late F. G. Edwards [Add. MS 41570 and Egerton MSS 3090-92]', *British Museum Quarterly*, VII, 1933, 30-1.

Schofield, Bertram, 'The Perabo Collection of musical Autographs, [Add. MSS 41628-35. Including autographs of works by J. S. Bach, Haydn, Schubert and Weber and letters by Brahms, Liszt, Mozart, Mendelssohn, Robert and Clara Schumann]', *British Museum Quarterly*, III, 1928-9, 56-7.

Schofield, Bertram, 'The Provenance and Date of "Sumer is icumen in" [Harley MS 978]', *Music Review*, IX, 1948, 81-6.

Schofield, Bertram, 'Rossini's Stabat Mater [Add. MS 43970]', *British Museum Quarterly*, X, 1936, 109-10.

Schofield, Bertram, and Dart, Thurston, 'Tregian's Anthology [Egerton MS 3665]', *Music & Letters*, 38, 1951, 205-216.

Schofield, Bertram, and Wilson, (Sir) A. Duncan, 'Some new Beethoven Letters [Add. MS 41628, ff.30-35]', *Music & Letters*, 21, 1939, 235-41.

Schofield, Bertram, and Wright, C. E., 'The Meyerstein Bequest [Add. MSS 47843-62, music]', *British Museum Quarterly*, XVII, 1953, 97-100.

Searle, Arthur, 'Haydn Autographs and "authentic" manuscript Copies in the British Library', *Early Music*, 10, 1982, 495-504.

Smith, William C., 'Two Songs of Handel [Add. MS 31993 ff.46b,48]', *British Museum Quarterly*, XII, 1938, 53-5.

Smithers, Don, 'Seventeenth century English trumpet Music [Add. MS 49599]', *Music & Letters*, 48, 1967, 358-65.

Staehlein, Martin, 'Eine florentiner Musikhandschrift aus der Zeit um 1500. Quellen-kundliche Bermerkungen zur Frottola-Sammlung MS. Egerton 3051 des British Museum und zum "Wolfheim-Manuscript" der Library of Congress [showing the two fragments to have belonged originally to the same MS]', *Schweizer Beiträge zur Musikwissenschaft*, I, 1972, 55-81.

Tilmouth, Michael 'Revision in the Chamber Music of Matthew Locke [Add. MS 17801]', *Proceedings of the Royal Musical Association*, 98, 1971-2, 89-100.

Tirro, Frank, 'Royal 8. G.vii: Strawberry leaves, single arch, and wrong-way lions', *Musical Quarterly*, LXVII, 1981, 1-28.

Tyson, Alan, 'New Light on Mozart's "Prussian" Quartets [Add. MS 37765]', *Musical Times*, 106, 1975, 126-30.

Tyson, Alan, 'The Origins of Mozart's "Hunt" Quartet, K458 [Add. MS 37763, ff.45-57b]', *Music and Bibliography*, edited by O. W. Neighbour, 1980, 132-48.

Tyson, Alan, 'A Reconstruction of the Pastoral Symphony Sketchbook [British Museum Add. MS 31766]', *Beethoven Studies: edited by Alan Tyson*, Oxford University Press, 1974, 67-97.

Willetts, Pamela, 'Autograph Manuscripts of Sir Arnold Bax [Add. MSS 50173-81]', *British Museum Quarterly*, XXIII, 1960-61, 43-5.

Willetts, Pamela, 'An autograph Manuscript of Percy Grainger [Add. MS 50823, P.F. arrangement of *Country Gardens*]', *British Museum Quarterly*, XXV, 1962, 18-19.

Willetts, Pamela, 'Autographs of Angelo Notari [chiefly Add. MS 46378B]', *Music & Letters*, 50, 1969, 124-6.

Willetts, Pamela, 'Autographs of Musicians [Egerton MS 3722, a certificate signed by William Byrd: Add. MS 48590 I and K, letters of Thomas Lupo and C. V. von Gluck; Add. MS 48369 first sketch of Holst's choral fantasia]', *British Museum Quarterly*, XX, 1955, 3-4.

Willetts, Pamela, 'The Ayrton Papers: music in London, 1786-

1858 [Add. MS 60358-60381]', *British Library Journal*, 6, 1980, 7-23.

Willetts, Pamela, 'The Dohnányi Collection [Add. MSS 50790-820]', *British Museum Quarterly*, XXV, 1961, 3-11.

Willetts, Pamela, *The Henry Lawes Manuscript.* [Add. MS 53723.] pp.ix.83. pl.xxii. 1969.

Willetts, Pamela, 'The Memoirs of Dr. Burney [Add. MS 48345]', *British Museum Quarterly*, XIX, 1954, 72-3.

Willetts, Pamela, 'Music from the Circle of Anthony Wood at Oxford [Add. MSS 17792-6]', *British Museum Quarterly*, XXIV, 1960, 71-5.

Willetts, Pamela, 'A neglected Source of Monody and Madrigal [Add. MS 31440]', *Music & Letters*, 43, 1962, 329-39.

Willetts, Pamela, 'The Percy Grainger Collection [Add. MSS 50867-9]', *British Museum Quarterly*, XXVII, 1963, 65-71.

Willetts, Pamela, 'The Ralph Vaughan Williams Collection [Add. MSS 50361-482]', *British Museum Quarterly*, XXIV, 1960, 3-11.

Willetts, Pamela, 'Recent British Museum Acquisitions' [on autographs of Vaughan Williams, Dohnányi, William Baines, Bax, Benjamin Dale, etc.], *Musical Times*, 102, 1961, 287.

Willetts, Pamela, 'The Rutland Boughton Collection [Add. MSS 50960-51012]', *British Museum Quarterly*, XXVIII, 1964, 67-75.

Willetts, Pamela, 'Silvanus Stirrop's Book [part of Add. MS 56279]', *Royal Musical Association Research Chronicle*, 10, 1972, 101-7. Addendum – *Royal Musical Association Research Chronicle*, 12, 1974, 156.

Willetts, Pamela, 'Sir Nicholas Le Strange and John Jenkins [chiefly on Add. MSS 39550-4]', *Music & Letters*, 42, 1961, 30-43.

Willetts, Pamela, 'Sir Nicholas Le Strange's Collection of Masque Music [Add. MS 10444]', *British Museum Quarterly*, XXIX, 1965, 79-81.

Willetts, Pamela, 'Vaughan Williams' Symphony in F minor [Add. MS 50140]', *British Museum Quarterly*, XXIII, 1960-61, 6.

DEPARTMENT OF ORIENTAL MANUSCRIPTS AND PRINTED BOOKS

THE CATALOGUES

Each of the catalogues of this department is devoted to the literature of a single language or a group of related languages. The catalogues are listed summarily in:

> *Guide to the Department of Oriental Manuscripts and Printed Books.* Compiled by H. J. Goodacre and A. P. Pritchard. British Library, 1977.

This *Guide* includes both the published catalogues, and those maintained in 'blue-slip' form for consultation within the department. Almost all the published catalogues have a subject index. The following pages list the titles of those whose index includes 'music' in the widest sense of the term. Here the works are set out according to the various headings – author, editor, or anonymous title – under which the full entry for each can be found in the body of the catalogue. Many entries include a summary in English. In the list, the relevant reference to pages or columns is given after the date of publication. The catalogues are listed in a geographical sequence which, broadly speaking, follows that in the above *Guide.* Besides the departmental catalogues, two volumes in the *Repertoire internationale des sources musicales* (*RISM*) are also mentioned.

Near and Middle East

Catalogue of Arabic Books in the British Museum. By A. G. Ellis. 2 vol. 1984, 1901. Vol.3, Indexes, by A. S. Fulton, 1935. Section 9, col.280.

Catalogue of Arabic printed Books in the British Museum. Compiled by A. S. Fulton and A. G. Ellis. 1926, col.1011-1014.

Second supplementary Catalogue of Arabic printed Books in the British Museum. By Alexander S. Fulton and Martin Lings. 1959. col.1057.

Third supplementary Catalogue of Arabic printed Books

in the British Library 1958-1969. By Martin Lings and Yasim Hamid Safadi. 1977. vol.IV, pp.447-50.

Catalogus codicum manuscriptorum orientalium qui in museo britannico asservantur. Pars secunda codices arabicos amplectens. [Begun by William Cureton, completed by Charles Rieu.] 1871. p.875.

Supplement to the Catalogue of Arabic Manuscripts in the British Museum. By Charles Rieu. 1894. pp.558-61.

Descriptive List of the Arabic Manuscripts acquired by the Trustees of the British Museum since 1894. By A. G. Ellis and Edward Edwards. 1912. p.55.

The Theory of Music in Arabic Writings (c.900-1900). Descriptive catalogue of manuscripts in the libraries of Europe and the USA. By Amnon Shiloah. G. Henle: München, 1979. (*Repertoire internationale des sources musicales. RISM* B X.) Enumerates, on pp.30-32 of the preliminary list, sixty-two MSS in the Department of Oriental Manuscripts and Printed Books in the British Library.

Catalogue of Georgian and other Caucasian printed Books in the British Museum. By David Marshall Lang. 1962. col.411.

Hebrew Writings concerning Music. In manuscripts and printed books from Geonic times up to 1800. By Israel Adler. G. Henle: München, 1975. (*Repertoire internationale des sources musicales. RISM* B IX^2.) Enumerates, on pp.xlii,xliii of the preliminary list of contents, twenty-seven MSS in the Department of Oriental Manuscripts and Printed Books in the British Library. (The departmental *Catalogue of Hebrew Books in the Library of the British Museum* by J. Zedner, 1867, and *Catalogue of Hebrew Books acquired during the years 1868-1892*, by S. van Straalen, 1894, both contain works of music and musical literature, but lack subject indexes.)

A Catalogue of Persian printed Books in the British Museum. By Edward Edwards. 1922. col.870.

Handlist of Persian Manuscripts 1895-1966. By G. M. Meredith-Owens. 1968. pp.32-3.

Miniatures from Persian Manuscripts. A catalogue and

subject index of paintings from Persia, India and Turkey in the British Library and British Museum. By Norah M. Titley. pp.xii. 359. pl.41. British Library, 1977.

Under the heading 'musical instruments', the index includes references to some forty instruments and groups, such as Bagpipes, Bells, Castanets, *Chagāneh*, (bowed instrument), *Chang* (harp), Cymbals, *Dhol* (drum), Drums, Flutes, *Ghichak* (spike fiddle), Harp, Horns, Kettledrum, Lutes, Musical boxes, *Nai* (end-blown flute), Orchestras, Organ, Panpipes, *Rabab* (fiddle), *Tabla* (drum), Trumpets, Zither. Under 'musicians' there are references to over 200 representations of performance.

A number of Turkish manuscripts in the British Library and in the British Museum (albums in the Department of Oriental Antiquities) include representations of instruments and performance. The manuscripts date from the sixteenth century to the eighteenth. They are included in:

Miniatures from Turkish Manuscripts. A catalogue and subject index of paintings in the British Library and British Museum. By Norah M. Titley. pp.144. pl.54. British Library, 1981.

References to musicians will be found in the 'Index of occupations and ranks'. The 'Index of musical instruments' includes references to: *Bara* (trumpet), Bells, *Çenk* (harp), *Çevğan* (jingling johnny), *Davul* (drum), *Def* (frame-drum), *Ikitelli* (two-stringed lute), *Kemençe* (Black Sea violin), Lutes, Musical box, *Nakare* (kettledrum), *Ney* (end-blown flute), *Sesţar* (six-stringed lute), *Zil* (cymbals), *Zurna* (shawm).

South Asia

A supplementary Catalogue of Bengali Books in the Library of the British Museum acquired during the years 1881-1910. By J. F. Blumhardt. 1910. col.387-88.

Second supplementary Catalogue of Bengali Books in the library of the British Museum acquired during the years 1911-34. By the late J. F. Blumhardt and J. V. S. Wilkinson. 1939. col.592.

Catalogue of Hindi . . . printed Books in the Library of the British Museum. By J. F. Blumhardt. 1893. col.254.

A supplementary Catalogue of Hindi Books in the Library of the British Museum, acquired during the years 1893-1912. By J. F. Blumhardt. 1913. col.425-26.

Second supplementary Catalogue of printed Books in Hindi, Bihari and Pahari in the Library of the British Museum. By L. D. Barnett, J. F. Blumhardt and J. V. S. Wilkinson. 1957. col.1437-9.

Catalogue of the Malayalam Books in the British Museum. By Albertine Gaur. 1971. col.503.

Catalogue of Marathi and Gujarati printed Books in the British Museum. By J. F. Blumhardt. 1892. col.185.

A supplementary Catalogue of Marathi and Gujarati printed Books in the British Museum. By J. F. Blumhardt. 1915. col.300.

Catalogue of Sanskrit, Pali and Prakrit Books in the British Museum, acquired during the years 1876-92. By Cecil Bendall. 1893. col.613 (music, dancing, etc.).

Ditto . . . acquired during the years 1892-1906. By L. D. Barnett. 1908. col.1031.

Ditto . . . acquired during the years 1906-28. By L. D. Barnett. 1928. col.1518 ('music, dancing and actor's art').

Catalogue of the Sinalese printed Books in the British Museum. By Don Martino de Zilva Wickremasinghe. 1901. col.278.

A Catalogue of the Tamil Books in the Library of the British Museum. By L. D. Barnett and the late G. U. Pope. 1909. col.539-40.

A supplementary Catalogue of Tamil Books in the Library of the British Museum. By L. D. Barnett. 1931. col.611-2.

The index of a second supplementary catalogue of Tamil books, by Albertine Gaur (in course of preparation 1981), contains references both for music and musical literature.

Catalogue of Telugu Books in the Library of the British Museum. By L. D. Barnett. 1912. col.399 ('music and actor's art').

[Urdu] *Catalogue of Hindustani printed Books in the Library of the British Museum.* By J. F. Blumhardt. 1889.

The subject-index is selective. Under 'Arts and games' it

includes 'cricket' but excludes musical subjects. There are however some important books on the sitār, viz:

Muḥammad Ṣafdar Ḥusaim Khan: *Qānūn-i sitār.* [Rules for playing the Sitār.] pp.iv.278. Lucknow, [1871?].

Ḥasan, Sayyid: *Rāgāmālā.* [Instructions on the Use of the Sitār.] pp.144. Delhi, 1876.

Rahīm Beg: *Naghmah-yi sitār.* [The Sitār, and how to play it.] pp.181. Lahore, 1876.

Rahīm Beg: *Tashil al-sitār.* [Instructions for playing the Sitār.] pp.108. Cawnpore, 1874.

[Urdu] *A supplementary Catalogue of Hindustani Books in the Library of the British Museum acquired during the years 1889-1908.* By J. F. Blumhardt. 1909. col.624.

Far East

An alphabetical Index to the Chinese Encyclopedia Ch'in Ting Ku Chin T'u Shu Chi Ch'êng. By Lionel Giles. 1911.

The headings related to music are: ballads; ceremonial music in general; musical instruments; songs, collections of.

THE SCOPE OF THE COLLECTIONS

Near and Middle East

Arabic

All the Arabic manuscripts in the collections are fully described in RISM B X, *The Theory of Music in Arabic Writings*, listed above (p.120). A smaller part of the British Library's holding is summarily catalogued in: H. G. Farmer, 'The Sources of Arabian Music: a bibliography of Arabic MSS which deal with the theory, practice and history of Arabian music', *Records of the Glasgow Bibliographical Society*, XIII, 1939, 1-97. Some noteworthy manuscripts are:

Add. 23391, ff.21-25 (Farmer 98) *Sa'nat al zānin.* (The Construction of the Wind-Instrumentalist, ie an instrument winded by hydraulic pressure.) By Abulluniyis (ascribed erroneously to Apollonius of Perga). Translated 9th century.

Or. 136, ff.18v-32 (Farmer 201) *Kitāb al-adawī.* (The Book of the musical Modes.) By Safī al-Dīn, d.1294.

Or. 1535, ff.57-76v (Farmer 289) *Kitāb fī ma'rifat al-anghām wa'l-ḍurub* (The Book concerning the Knowledge of the Melodies and Rhythms). Anonymous. 17th century?

Or. 2361, ff.168v-219v (Farmer 260) [*Kitāb lī Muḥammad ibn Murāk fi'l-mūsīqī* (The Muḥammad ibn Murād Book on Music)]. Anonymous. 15th century.

Or. 2361, ff.236v-38v (Farmer 123). *Risala fi'l-mūsīqī* (The Treatise about Music). By Al-Munnijjim, d.912. 10th century.

Or. 3138, ff.49-51v (Farmer 37) *Kitāb fī Tabaqāt al-mughannīn* (The Book about the Ranks of the Singers). By Al-Jāṇiẓ. 9th century.

Or. 6629 (Farmer 247) *Risālat al-fathīya fi'l-mūsīqī* (The Treatise of Profit concerning Music). By Al-Lādhiqī, d.1445. 15th century.

Or. 9649, ff.1v-5 (Farmer 100) *Risala ṣan'at al-urghīn al-būqī* (The Treatise on the Construction of the Pipe Organ). By 'Morisitos' ('Mūrisṭus'). Translated 9th century.

Or. 9649, ff.6v-11 (Farmer 99) *Risala san'at al-urghīn al-zamri* (The Treatise on the Construction of the Reed-Pipe Organ). By 'Morisitos' ('Mūrisṭus'). Translated 9th century.

Or. 9649, ff.11v-13 (Farmer 101) *Risala ṣan'at al juljal* (The Treatise on the Construction of the Chime). By 'Morisitos' ('Mūrisṭus'). Translated 9th century.

Or. 13019 Risālat aṣ-Saidāwī (The Treatise . . .) [A general treatise on music]. By Aṣ-Saidāwī. Early 14th century.

Armenian

The Armenian collection includes two manuscripts of importance in the history of notation. These are:

[A hymn-book of the Armenian church.] 1435. Or. 8999.

[A 'Šaraknoc'', a book of hymns of the Armenian church, with illuminated titles and initials.] 1312. Add. MS 18603.

Both these contain in the text the *xaz* (neumatic) system of notation (see Komitas Keworkian – later known as Father Komitas – 'Die armenische Kirchenmusik', *Sammelbände der Internationalen Musikgesellschaft*, I, 1899, 54-64), which dates from the fifth century AD. After the key to the understanding of this notation was lost in the eighteenth century, a new system was devised, c.1815, by H. Limonjian. Two important books of religious music notated in this system are:

P. Nikołayos and S. T'aščean, *J̌aynagreal Šarakan hogewor ergoc'*, Ejmiacin, 1875. 17024.f.1.

Anon. *Ergk' ǰaynagrealk'i Žamagroc*, Ejmiacin, 1877. 17068.f.7.

An important two-volume collection of Armenian folk-songs is Komitas's:

Zołovrdakan erger, edited by S. Melik'yan, Erejan, 1931, 32. 17068.f.1,2.

The department also contains a collection of books about Armenian music. Some collections of Armenian folk-music are entered in the *Catalogue of printed Music in the British Library to 1980*, under the heading 'Komitas, Father'.

Hebrew

The following are selected references to illustrations of musical instruments in manuscripts and printed books.

Manuscripts

(a) Ram's horns (*shofarot*) in illustrations of Temple vessels:
Add. MS 15250 (14th-15th century) f.4r.
Harl. MS 1528 (probably 13th to 14th century) f.8r.
Kings MS, 1 (1384-1385) f.4r.

(b) David and his harp:
Add. MS 11639 (13th century) f.117v.
Add. MS 15282 (13th-14th century) f.302r.
Harl. MS 5713 (1714) f.4r (including also trumpets).

(c) Trumpets, mostly angelic:
Add. MS 14761 (14th century) ff.17v,52r.

(d) Trumpet and bagpipe:
Add. MS 14761 (14th century) f.64r (with bells, rebec, mandore (?), and drums).

(e) Musicians:
Add. MS 14761 (14th century) f.61r.
Harl. MS 5713 (1714) f.4v (music-teacher and pupil, with players on zither and violin).

(f) Hunting horn:
Or. 5024 (1374) f.78r.

(g) Ram's horn (*shofar*) being played as part of a synagogue ritual:
Harl. MS 5713 (1714) f.10r.
Add. MS 26928 (1383) ff.244r, 248r, 251v.

Printed books

(a) Hunting horn:
Haggadoh, Augsburg, 1534. C.49.b.7, ff.5,6.

(b) Ram's horn (*shofar*) in synagogue ritual:
Krobes, Amsterdam, 1671. 1971.e.3, f.1v.

(c) Music of Passover hymns (the earliest printed?):
Liber Rituum Paschalium, Regiomonti, 1644. 1974. c.8 passim.

The Hebrew collections also include the alto part of:
Salomone Rossi, [*Ha-Shirim Asher Li'Shlomo,*] Venice, 1623. 1997.g.7.

Persian

For Persian manuscripts with miniatures of musical subjects, *see* the descriptive catalogue by Norah Titley listed above (p.121).

Turkish

For Turkish manuscripts with miniatures of musical subjects, *see* the descriptive catalogue by Norah Titley listed above (p.121).

South Asia

Sanskrit, etc.

The following are some manuscripts which contain illustrations of various kinds showing musical performance:

A Sanskrit manuscript, containing part of the Skanda of the Bhāgavāta-purāna, dealing with the childhood of Krishna, written on palm leaves. With illustrations. 16th century. Or. 11689.

An album containing thirty-five fine paintings illustrating the musical Rāgas, with descriptive Hindi verses. 17th century. Or. 8838.

An album of thirty-six paintings of the Rāgas and Rāginīs, with descriptive Hindi verses. 18th century. Or. 8839.

The Ramāyāna, books I, II, IV, VI, illustrated with coloured drawings in Indian style. 1763, 1707-10. Add. MSS 15295-97.

South East Asia

Burmese

An illustrated Burmese folding manuscript, depicting the royal procession of King Mindon, contains numerous fine illustrations of Burmese musicians – drum circles, gong circles, etc. Second half of the 19th century. Or. 12013.

Literature

Charles Duroiselle, *Pageant of King Mindon . . . (1865)*. [A selection from Or. 12013, with explanatory text.] Calcutta, 1925. (Memoirs of the Archaeological Survey of India. no.27.) Some of the fifteen plates include musical participants.

Another manuscript, a portfolio of miniatures representing scenes in the Romance of Ī-naung, includes pictures of Burmese harp playing. 19th century. Or. 3676. fol.19.

Far East

Chinese

The following is a selection of manuscripts of musical interest (many of the dates are only approximate):

Musical notation of the tune 'Chou Jian'. 18th century. Add. MS 6653.
A manual on lute playing, with diagrams on p.8 and p.13. 19th century. Add. MS 16327.

Volumes of illustrations of the lives of the Miao people (in the Yunnan province of south-west China), including a number of illustrations of performers with instruments:
Add. MS 16594. 19th century?

f.13 One *san-hsien* (long lute), with a player of a small wooden block.
f.23 One *sheng*-type mouth organ; with two players of *lings* (little bells for horses).
f.31 One *so-on* (conical oboe); one small drum, suspended round the neck of the player; one *po* (cymbals); one *lo* (gong).

Add. MS 16595. 19th century?

f.34 One *lo* (gong); one *sheng*-type mouth organ; with one player of *lings* (little bells for horses).

Or. 2262. 19th century.

f.99 One player of *kuai ban* (clappers).

Or. 4153. c.1810.

f.8 One small drum, held upright; one *so-on* (conical oboe); with two players of *lings*.
f.9 Three *sheng*-type mouth organs.
f.25 One *sheng*-type mouth organ.
f.30 Two *sheng*-type mouth organs.

Or. 5005. c.1840. Described on cover as 'Eighteen coloured drawings of the Meaon-Tsze'.

f.2 Three players, with two sticks each, sitting round a drum on the ground.
f.8 One *sheng*-type mouth organ.

Or. 7360. Early 19th century – pre-1815. The life of Confucius illustrated in line drawings, some of which show him either listening to instruments or playing them himself. (The drawings are not uniformly clear in detail).

f.4 Two *ch'in* (zither).
f.6 One *ch'in* (zither).
f.7 One *po-chung* (bell in a frame); one *t'ê-ching* (stone gong); two *ch'in* (zither).

f.27 One *ch'in* (zither).
f.44 One *ch'in* (zither); one *pi-pa* (lute).
ff.72,73,76 One *ch'in* (zither) on each.

Or. 9623. 19th century. (Including illustrations of the Lolo people's customs.)

f.2 Four *sheng*-type mouth organs.
f.6 Four *sheng*-type mouth organs; with one player of the *lings* (little bells for horses).
f.8 Three players of *lings* (little bells for horses).
f.11 One *liuli laba* (glass trumpet); one *so-on* (conical oboe); one *tao-ku* (barrel drum) (?) supported on a pole.
f.21 Two *sheng*-type mouth organs.
f.28 One *liuli laba* (glass trumpet); one *po* (cymbals); one small, horizontal drum.
f.54 Two *sheng*-type mouth organs.
f.55 Three players round one drum on the ground.

Or. 11513. c.1850.

f.2 Procession of three *sheng*-type mouth organ players, with three players of *lings* (little bells for horses).
f.7 Two *so-on* (conical oboe); one tambourine; one *lo* (gong).

Or. 11539. 19th century.

f.33 One *pang-ku* (drum on a tripod).
f.100 One *k'ou chin* (chinese jew's harp).
f.131 Several *liuli laba* (glass trumpets).
f.132 *Feng-xiao* (bamboo whistles) for attaching to pigeons' tails, to frighten hawks.

Or. 11694. 19th century (?). Portraits of Lohans (disciples of the Buddha).

f.7 Lohan on a tiger ringing a *to* (hand-bell).

An important printed source of musical information is the Ch'ing dynasty encyclopedia *Ch'in Ting Ku Chin T'u Shu Chi Ch'êng*, principally compiled by Ch'en Meng-lei (b.1651). [Peking, late seventeenth to early eighteenth century]. 15023.b.1. Section 29 deals with music. For illustrations, see Chuan (chapter) 55-58, 83-96, 97-124. For the index, see p.123 above. A smaller encyclopedia was compiled by Wang-ch'i (c.1535-1620) and is entitled *San cai tu hui*,

1690 reprinted c.1830. 15024.c.1. Section 35, dealing with the arts, includes illustrations of musical instruments, some of which are imaginary rather than factual.

The Music Library in the Department of Printed Books has a small quantity of modern Chinese music, both vocal (pressmark G.1363) and instrumental (pressmark g.1470-1474).

Japanese

A rare printed book of Japanese music is:

> Kunkunshi. Gekan. (Eighty-seven pieces of Ryukyuan music for the *samisen*, printed in Kunkunshi notation. With a two-page postface in Chinese, signed by Chinjō Atsumi and Fusō Senro.) vol.3 ff.66. (2). Nakamoto Chō [boku?]: Teishiraji [Okinawa, late eighteenth century?]. Or. 74.cc.4.

Possibly printed from moveable type, this may therefore be one of the earliest examples of moveable type printing in Okinawa.

The Music Library in the Department of Printed Books has a small quantity of twentieth century Japanese music, both vocal (pressmark G.1362) and instrumental (pressmark g.819).

SCIENCE REFERENCE LIBRARY

Holborn Branch (25 Southampton Buildings, London WC2)

This section of the Reference Division (formerly known as the Patent Office Library) contains material of great importance for the history of the development of musical technology of all kinds.

The earliest printed volume of musical patents is:
Patents for Inventions. Abridgements of specifications relating to music and musical instruments. A.D. 1694-1861. [The preface signed: B. Woodcroft.] pp.x.374. 1864.

This, like all subsequent volumes listed here, was issued by the Patent Office. Its contents were subsumed into the first part of the following:

Patents for Inventions. (Class 26.) Abridgements of specifications relating to music and musical instruments. A.D. 1694-1866. Second edition. [part I] pp.xiv.520. 1871. [part II] pp.ix.246. A.D. 1867-1876. [1881].

After this, the class was altered from 26 to 88, and volumes appeared at fairly frequent intervals.

Patents for inventions. Abridgements of specifications. Class 88, music and musical instruments. Period – A.D. 1855-1866. pp.xi.96. 1905.

ditto *Period – A.D. 1867-76.* pp.xi.101. 1904.

ditto *Period – A.D. 1877-83.* pp.x.77. 1893.

ditto *Period – A.D. 1884-88.* pp.xii.137. 1896.

ditto *Period – A.D. 1889-92.* pp.xii.103. 1898.

ditto *Period – A.D. 1893-96.* pp.xii.131. 1900.

ditto *Period – A.D. 1897-1900.* pp.xii.135. 1903.

ditto *Period – A.D. 1901-4.* pp.xiv.187. 1907.

ditto *Period – A.D. 1905-8.* pp.xv.227. 1911.

ditto *Class 88 (i). Musical instruments, automatic. Period – A.D. 1909-15.* pp.viii.162. 1921.

ditto *Class 88 (i). Musical instruments, automatic. Period – A.D. 1916-20.* pp.v.35. 1925.

ditto. *Class 88 (i). Musical instruments, automatic. Period – A.D. 1921-25.* pp.vi.52. 1929.

ditto *Class 88 (i). Musical instruments, automatic. Period – A.D. 1926-30.* pp.v.22. 1932.

ditto *Class 88 (ii). Music and musical instruments other than automatic. Period – A.D. 1921-25.* pp.xi.91. 1929.

ditto *Class 88 (ii). Music and musical instruments other than automatic. Period – A.D. 1926-30.* pp.xi.80. 1933.

In all the volumes listed above as 'class 88', patents for various peripheral aspects of music are not included, but are covered in the indexes by means of references to other subjects. For instance:

Music: binders, temporary. *See Abridgement Class Writing Instruments &c.*

By the third decade of the twentieth century, the rapidly increasing use of electricity in the production of musical sound of all kinds widened the range of technology, and consequently affected the way in which the relevant patents were classified.

After 1930 abridgements of specifications for musical patents ceased to be published as a separate class. Class 88 (comprising, as hitherto, 'Musical instruments, automatic' and 'Music and musical instruments, other than automatic') was then issued as 'Group XXXVIII', 'Music, phonographs, signals and alarms'. The first volume of this group appeared in 1932: in it the abridgements are listed in numerical sequence, irrespective of subject, but musical items can be traced through the index. The last volume of 'Group XXXVIII', with the above subtitle, appeared in 1961. In the volume issued in 1962, 'Group XXXVIII' was subtitled 'Music, gramophones, signalling', a description which continued for two more volumes, both issued in 1963. Thereafter, this series was discontinued, and abridgements of patent specifications for music were allocated to G5 within the Group G4-G6, itself included in an annual general series. Precise references can be found in the two series: 'Key to the classification divisions', and 'Reference index to the classification key'.

Part II

BRITISH MUSEUM

INTRODUCTION

As indicated in the Foreword (p.ix), the several departments of the Museum contain a notable variety of documents and objects of musical interest. Some are to be found in published catalogues which describe a particular collection, or record objects of a special type or period. Many others are included in unpublished catalogues of various kinds. Certain objects or groups have been described in special monographs. In this book, it hardly seemed practicable to do more than give selective information. Most of the objects separately listed in the following pages are followed by a registration number, which serves for identification. It usually consists of a year followed by a figure or sequence of figures, each separated by a dash or a point or a combination of the two, for instance, 1974-4-12-1. There are a few exceptions in which, for instance, instead of the year there stands first the name or initials of the donor or collector, such as 'Christy' (Oriental Antiquities), or 'Sloane' (Prints and Drawings), or 'CAI' (Mediaeval and Later). In the Department of Prints and Drawings identification may also be provided by an abridged catalogue reference: for certain items, published in book form with a title, a shelfmark is given.

The sequence in which the nine Museum departments are arranged calls perhaps for some comment. They are grouped implicitly into two categories, the first five being – broadly speaking – 'European' departments, the last four 'non-European'. The Department of Prints and Drawings stands at the head of the first group because the general character of the items of musical interest in its collections has such a close material affinity with the holdings of the Reference Division of the British Library.

One important official publication of general interest may be mentioned here: *Music and Civilisation.* (Edited by Terence Mitchell.) pp.247. 1980. (The British Museum Yearbook 4.) The ten articles in this yearbook, written by specialists who are mostly members or former members of the British Museum's staff, are supplied with 173 illustrations, and describe particular objects or groups of objects in the collections, in some cases relating them to others elsewhere. The title of each article is listed under 'literature' at the end of the section devoted to the relevant department. The editor's introduction gives a most valuable summary of the musical objects in the Museum's collections, the instruments being classified according to the system of sound production, a method which is broadly adopted, as appropriate, in the following pages.

Another special issue of a journal is that of *World Archaeology*, vol.12, no.3, which is subtitled 'Archaeology and musical Instruments', edited by Vincent Megaw and Ian Longworth. Four of its ten articles allude to instruments in the Museum's collections, and each is listed under the relevant department.

DEPARTMENT OF PRINTS AND DRAWINGS

These collections are primarily devoted to the fine arts and certain of the applied arts, as they have developed in western civilization, mostly arranged according to artist or engraver. This is generally reflected in the small part of the collection which is covered by the published catalogues, with the exception of those devoted to special subjects such as fans and playing cards, in which the products of several countries are brought together.

A good many of the published catalogues include indexes with references to depictions of musicians and musical subjects. Other prints and drawings in this field can be traced through the various working catalogues available in the Students' Room.

THE CATALOGUES, ETC.

Some published catalogues containing a significant quantity of items of musical interest are (in chronological order):

A descriptive Catalogue of Playing and other Cards in the British Museum. By William Hughes Willshire. 1876, reprinted 1975.

It includes:

G.133. Twelve cards from a numerical series of fifty-two, printed in Germany, 17th century. The back of each card bears a three-stave musical score.

E.206. Forty-eight cards from a set of fifty-two, printed in London, c.1740. Most cards have four lines of music, followed by a song with flute accompaniment.

Further information is given in: Armstrong, Clifford, '16th century German playing Cards: a little known source of German song [referring *inter alia* to Willshire G.133,135, and to Schreiber G.3]', *Early Music*, 3, 1977, 209-17.

A Catalogue of Maps, Plans and Views of London, Westminster & Southwark. Collected and arranged by Frederick Crace. Edited by his son John Gregory Crace. 1878.

Arranged by areas, in portfolios. Portfolios XI-XIV, XVII, XVIII, XXIX, XXX, XXXII, XXXV, contain numerous views of opera houses, theatres, halls and other buildings associated with music, of special structures such as those erected for Handel's Fireworks Music of 1749, and of the various pleasure gardens.

Catalogue of the Collection of Fans and Fan Leaves presented to the British Museum by the Lady Charlotte Schreiber. Compiled by Lionel Cust. 1893.

The following are of musical interest:

Mounted fans:

6 The Royal Concert. Compiled from an engraving by John Barlow after a drawing by I. Cruikshank, entitled: 'Representation of a Royal Concert at Buckingham House. Publish'd as the Act directs, 16 Octr 1781, by J. Preston'.

27 Concert on the Water. Etching coloured by hand.

32 The Harp. Stipple engraving.

43 Plan of the King's Theatre for 1788. Etching.

48 Dance Fan, 1792. Ten country dances, four strathspeys and four reels for the year 1792. Etching.

50 Dance Fan, 1793. Includes the music of ten country dances and five cotillons. John Cock & Crowder: [London,] 1793.

51 Dance Fan, 1794. Caricatures of dancing. With the music of fourteen dances. Stokes, Scott & Crosby: [London,] 1794.

61 New Dance Fan for 1797. Includes the music of sixteen dances. (1797.)

62 New Opera Fan. 1797. Publish'd as the Act directs ... by permission of Manager of the Opera House, 42 Pall Mall.

Unmounted fan lc

91 Three female figures playing harps and tambourine.

92 A similar leaf.

129 The Minuet. [Two dancers.] Pub'^{d} Octr 5th 1782 by I. Cock.

131 The Lesson on the Spinet.

241 Five scenes from Rossini's opera of William Tell.

337 Figaro. Three scenes from Beaumarchais' play *Le mariage de Figaro*, with thirteen stanzas of verse, the first set to music, commencing 'Coeurs sensibles, coeurs fideles'.

Catalogue of the Collection of Playing Cards bequeathed to the Trustees of the British Museum by the late Lady Charlotte Schreiber. Compiled by Freeman M. O'Donoghue. 1901.

It includes:

English cards:

78 Dance music. [London? c.1775.] Two packs, each card bearing the music of a contredance. One pack comprises 51 cards (lacking the 2 of diamonds). The other comprises 24, larger, quadrille cards, with an instruction card giving the rules of 'Quadrille without pooling, as played at Bath'.

79 4 cards, containing songs, c.1730, complementary to Willshire 206.

143 & 144 The Musical Games of Pope Joan, Casino and Commerce. By E. E. Thomas. No.143 comprises 59 cards, giving keys, notes, and rests in all values, from semibreve to demisemiquaver. No.144 comprises 70 similar cards, with a pamphlet of instructions. Chappell: [London, c.1830.]

173 Paine of Almack's Quadrilles. 16 cards with French descriptions of dances. H. Falkner's Opera Warehouse: [London, c.1820.]

French cards:

176 'Douzieme jeu de cartes instructives. Musique. Ouvrage destiné à l'instruction de la jeunesse des deux sexes. A.-A. Renouard et Nicole: Paris, [c.1810.] Forty-eight cards, explaining the rudiments.

Catalogue of engraved British Portraits preserved in the Department of Prints and Drawings in the British Museum. By Freeman O'Donoghue (vol.1-4). By Freeman O'Donoghue and Henry M. Hake (vol.5. Groups). By Henry M. Hake (vol.6). 6 vol. 1908-25.

This catalogue includes numerous entries for musicians, most of which were abstracted by A. M. Hind into a manuscript card index. This index was copied by the Music Room of the British Museum c.1955, and the resultant cards were incorporated into the index of musical portraits found in its own collections (see p.49). Hind did not, however, make cards for the musicians in vol.5 of this catalogue ('Groups'). These are as follows:

p.28 The Prison Scene in Gay's *Beggar's Opera*, engraved by Blake, after Hogarth, 1790.

p.29 Scene in Bickerstaffe's *Love in a Village*, Act 1, scene 6. Engraved by J. Finlayson after J. Zoffany. n.d.

p.30 Scene in the musical entertainment *Lock and Key*, engraved by T. Lupton after G. Clint. 1824.

p.63 'The Musical Union, 1854', Heinrich Ernst, Henri Vieuxtemps, and Bernard Molique. Lithograph by C. Baugniet, after C. Baugniet.

p.63 'The Musical Union', 1851. 18 musicians, including Prosper Sainton, Henri Vieuxtemps, Heinrich Ernst, Henry Hill, Ferdinand Laub, Ernst Pauer, Carlo Piatti, Joseph Menter, Charles Hallé, W. Sterndale Bennett, and John Ella. Lithographed by C. Baugniet, after C. Baugniet.

p.63 'The Quartet'. Joachim, Louis Ries, Ludwig Straus and Alfredo Piatti. Etching by L. Loewenstam, after Lajos Bruck.

p.85 Frederick, Prince of Wales and family holding a musical party. c.1730. Etching by G. Cruikshank after M. Laroon.

p.89 Scene in Gilbert and Sullivan's *Patience.* Richard Temple, Frank T. Thornton and Durward Lely, singing the trio in Act 2. From a photograph.

p.95 A plaque, with portraits of Purcell, Blow, Croft, Arne and Boyce. Engraved by J. Drayton and R. Smirke.

Franks Bequest. Catalogue of British and American Bookplates bequeathed to the Trustees of the British Museum by Sir Augustus Wollaston Franks. By E. R. J. Gambier Howe. 3 vol. 1903,04.

Vol.III, pp.310-5, 'Circulating libraries', contains a number of bookplates etc., relating to music, as follows:

34259 Apollo Circulating Library and Music Warehouse, Worthing.
34300 Davenport, Oxford, Music Seller.
34308 Fitzpatrick Music and Musical Instrument Warehouse, Cork.
34310 Flack, Music Binder, Covent Garden.
34322 Hime, Dublin.
34374 Packer, Bath (late Lintern), Music Seller.
34380 Power, Dublin.
34417 Musical Instrument Seller, John Young.

Catalogue of early Italian Engravings preserved in the Department of Prints and Drawings in the British Museum, by Arthur Mayger Hind. Ed. by Sidney Colvin. vol. 1, 1910.

Pp.234-256 describe a set of 'Instructive Prints (erroneously called the "Tarocchi Cards of Mantegna"),' including: D.11-20, Apollo and the Muses, some of whom play musical instruments, and C.26, Music, also with instruments. The cards were probably designed at Ferrara, c.1467.

Catalogue of political and personal Satires preserved in the Department of Prints and Drawings in the British Museum. vol.v 1771-1783(–vol.xi 1828-1832). By M. Dorothy George. 1935-54.

The 'index of selected subjects' to each of these volumes contains a considerable wealth of musical material, under such headings as 'London, theatrical – King's Theatre, Lyceum, etc.', 'music', 'musical', 'musical – street performers'. There are also entries of musical significance in the 'index of persons', under such names as Paganini, Pasta, Braham, Clementi, Cramer, etc. The first four volumes of this catalogue (1870-1883), which cover the period 1320 to 1770, are by other authors and lack indexes. They contain few entries relevant to music, among which, however, are the two satirical portraits of Handel (attributed to Joseph Goupy), 1754, nos.3272, 3273 in vol.3, pt.2, and the so-called 'Uproar at Covent Garden', 1763, no.4004 in vol.4.

Catalogue of British Drawings. Vol.1: xvi & xvii centuries. By Edward Croft-Murray and Paul Hulton. 1970.

The index includes, among the group entitled 'miscellaneous', a score of references under 'musical instruments and musicians'.

Three other collections, of which there are no published catalogues, contain musical material. These are:

The Banks collection of admission tickets, formed by Sarah Sophia Banks (d.1818).

This includes numerous items relating to concert halls, opera houses, festivals and the like, in London and the provinces. A slip catalogue is available in the Students' Room of the Department.

The Banks collection of trade cards, formed by Sarah Sophia Banks (d.1818).

It includes some cards from the Franks collection and other sources. Section 88 of a manuscript catalogue, made by Andrew Parkinson in 1976, is devoted to music. It comprises 110 cards, of performers, music-sellers and publishers, teachers, and instrument makers. A copy of the entire catalogue is available in the Students' Room of the department.

The Heal collection of trade cards, formed by Sir Ambrose Heal (d.1959).

Section 88 of a manuscript list, made by Andrew Parkinson in 1976, is devoted to music. It comprises ninety-three cards, dating from c.1750 to c.1880, of performers, music-sellers and publishers, teachers and instrument makers. A copy of the entire catalogue is available in the Students' Room of the department, and a photocopy of section 88 is placed in the Music Library of the British Library at M.R. Ref. 3.d.

There is also a group of dated portrait drawings, in crayon, by Rudolf Lehmann (1819-1905). It is described in the article on him in the *Dictionary of National Biography* as the 'Album of Celebrities'. The musical subjects are:

Giuseppe Baini 1842
* Chopin 1847
H. W. Ernst 1851
* W. S. Gilbert 1893
* Gounod 1893
Ferdinand Hiller 1850
* Joachim 1851
* Lisa Lehmann
* Liszt 1849
Massenet 1893
* Meyerbeer 1860

Ignaz Moscheles 1850
* Clara Schumann 1860
Moritz von Schwind 1860
* Verdi 1884

Those portraits marked with an asterisk are reproduced in:
Men and Women of the Century. Being a collection of portraits and sketches by Mr. Rudolf Lehmann. Edited with introduction and short biographical notes by H. C. Marillier. pp.xxxi.78. 79 plates. George Bell & Sons: London, 1896. (Copy in the Department of Printed Books, Reference Division, British Library. Pressmark: K.T.C.42.b.6.)

The department also has a good many portraits, engraved or lithographed, which are not included in A. M. Hind's index (see pp.139-40). They can be traced, however, under the name of the subject, in the two blue-slip catalogues of portraits which are available in the Students' Room. One catalogue comprises English portraits, the other, which is subdivided by countries, foreign portraits.

SELECTED PRINTS AND DRAWINGS

The following is a selection, arranged, with one exception, under the artists' names, of various drawings, prints, volumes of prints, and volumes including prints, representing musicians, musical performance, etc.

Angelico, Fra (c.1400-1455)
The prophet David playing a psaltery. Pen and brown ink, on parchment. 1895-9-15-437.

Anonymous engraver
An English engraved roundel, c.1735, of a private rehearsal of an oratorio, with orchestra, choir and soloists, frequently described as 'Handel conducting an oratorio'. (This description, derived from a MS addition to a catalogue of prints sold by Edward Evans c.1850, has no authenticity.) 1856-7-12-210.

Anonymous scene-painter
A pen and water-colour drawing, c.1710, of the proscenium arch and stage-setting of the Queen's (later King's) Theatre, Haymarket, showing the stage on which most of Handel's operas were first performed. Burney collection, vol.i, no.101.

Anonymous water-colourist
A pavilion at Vauxhall Gardens, erected on a stage showing a pageant of figures in historical costume, with groups of musicians on the balconies. Water-colour. c.1845. 1982-2-27-7.

Archer, John Wykeham (1808-1864)
Covent Garden Theatre, after the fire of 1856. Three water-colours. Interior, looking to the stage. Interior, looking from the stage. East front. 1874-3-14-351,352,353.

Baugniet, Charles (1814-1886)
Sir Julius Benedict. c.1850. Half length water-colour portrait. 1892-4-25-1.

Beham, Hans Sebald (1500-1550)
Bagpiper and two pommer players. Engraving. B.VIII. 185. 166.
Drummer. Woodcut. C.D.I. 479. 148.
Fifer and drummer. Woodcut. 1543. B.VIII. 197. 198.
Fifer. Woodcut. C.D.I. 479. 149.
Violinist. Woodcut. 1520. C.D.I. 476. 141.

Bolten van Zwolle, Arent van (fl.c.1580-1600)
Italian carnival. Including players of lute, bagpipes, and shawm, with lute, tambourine and cornetts on the ground. Pen and brown ink. Sloane 5217-414.
Italian carnival. Including players of trumpet, bagpipes and shawm. Pen and brown ink. Sloane 5217-415.
A peasant merrymaking. Including bagpipe, shawm and dancers. Pen and brown ink. Sloane 5217-415.
Apollo and the muses. Including players of tambourine, lutes (3), bass viol, treble viol, harp, shawms (2) and harpsichord. Pen and brown ink. Sloane 5217-417.
Bagpiper and drummer with flageolet. Brush drawing. Sloane 5217-419.

Bagpiper and drummer with flageolet. Brush drawing. Sloane 5217-421.

Breu, Jorg, the younger (c.1510-1547)
Banquet in Venice, with fifer, drummer, violinist, mandoline player and dancers. Woodcut. c.1540. C.D.II. 434. 9.

Burgkmair, Hans, the elder (1473-1531)
Der Weiss Kunig. Eine Erzehlung von der Thaten Kaiser Maximilian des Ersten . . . nebst denen von Hanssen Burgkmair dazu verfertigten Holzschnitten. Auf Kosten Joseph Kurzbockens: Wien, 1775. 158.a.8.
28 'How the young White King learned to know music and stringed instruments'. A view of an interior, showing musicians apparently testing a positive organ, harp, virginals and cornett. On a table are a lira da braccio, crumhorn, flute and other wind instruments. On the floor are a marine trumpet, tabor and kettle-drum, a trombone and a lute-case. An earlier impression of this woodcut is at Case 44. XXIX.

Carmontelle, Louis Carrogis de (1717-1806)
Wolfgang Amadeus Mozart at the harpsichord, with his father Leopold behind him, and his sister 'Nannerl' behind the instrument. Watercolour, Paris, 1763/64. Deposited on permanent loan from the National Gallery 1955. BM 1972 U 653.
The same group, engraved by Jean Baptiste Delafosse after Carmontelle. Paris, 1764. 1925-2-14-4.

Carpaccio, Vittore (c.1460/5-1523/6)
Monk, with two lutenists, and one rebec-player. Drawing. c.1500. Shows the interior of a music room, with bow, viol, and (?) tambourine hanging on pegs from a shelf, and other instruments in the foreground. 1895-9-15-806.

Chalon, Alfred Edward (1780-1860)
'Cervetto aged 86. March 8th 1832'. Brush drawing over pencil. 1922-10-17-5.
Antonio Tamburini as 'Sir Riccardo Forth' in Bellini's *I Puritani.* Water-colour drawing. Probably a representation of this singer in the production at the King's Theatre in 1835. 1922-10-17.6.

Charlotte Tousez as Madame de Gervilliers in *Fanchon la vielleuse* [ie *Das Leyermädchen*, by F. A. Himmel], performed at the English Opera House 1829. Brush drawing over black chalk. 1922-10-17-2.
Recollections of the Italian Opera. Drawn on stone by R. J. Lane. John Mitchell: London, [1836-37?]. Includes Grisi as Desdemona, Pasta as Semiramide, Rubini as Arturo in *I Puritani*, Grisi as Anna Bolena, Tamburini as Riccardo, Grisi and Lablache in *I Puritani*, Grisi as Norma, Lablache as Faliero, Catoni Lonati as Nemorino in *L'Elisir d'amore.* 208.c.14.

Cock, Hieronymus (c.1510-1570)
Part of the funeral procession of Charles V. Fourteen trumpeters, preceded by two drummers. Pen and ink drawing. 1895-9-15-1017.

Crowquill, Alfred [ie Alfred Henry Forrester] (1800-72)
La tempesta . . . opera, in three acts, the music . . . by Halévy . . . composed for Her Majesty's Theatre, Haymarket. The scenery by Mr. Charles Marshall. Libretto by Scribe. [With six lithographs by M. and N. Hanhart, after A. Crowquill.] J. Mitchell, etc. [London.] 1850. 167.a.6.
Opera. Impressioni della [Marietta] Piccolomini. La Traviata. [Four lithographs of the first London production of Verdi's opera.] [1853?] 167.a.5.

Cruikshank, George (1792-1878)
'A little music à la française. Les savoyards'. Etching. Organist, singer and violinist in a street, with onlookers. 1818. Reid 779.
Portrait of Mr. Rutherford, pianoforte maker at Messrs Broadwoods. Pencil tinted with water colours. 1972. U. 556.

Duhameel, Albert (1449-c.1509)
Lute-player. Woodcut. W.II. 318.3. 1854-5-13-36.

Dürer, Albrecht (1471-1528)
Three musicians, playing lute, harp and fiddle. Drawing c.1515. Sloane 5218-131.
Portrait of a man, possibly Paul Hofhaimer. Drawing. 1518? Sloane 5218-52.

Flinck, Govaert (1615-1660)
Man seated, playing lute. Chalk drawing. 1895-9-15-1161.

Gainsborough, Thomas (1727-88)
Ann Ford, later Mrs Philip Thicknesse, holding a cittern. Water-colour over pencil. c.1760. (Miss Ford was a noted player of the musical glasses for which she published a method.) 1894-6-12-11.
'A music party'. Chalk drawing. c.1765. Harpsichord, violin and two singers. Stated in the verso (in a note signed 'Richard Lane', Gainsborough's nephew) to be 'Portraits of himself, his two daughters and Abel'. Abel, however, played the viola da gamba, not the violin. 1889-7-24-371.

Grieve, John Henderson (1770-1845)
Two water-colour scene sketches, probably for the 1800 revival of *The Woodman*, music by William Shield. 1956-7-14-5,6.
Water-colour sketch for *The Beacon of Liberty*, text by P. Bailey, music by Sir Henry Bishop, produced at Covent Garden, 1823. 1956-7-14-8.

Hayter, John (1800-after 1891)
Sketches of Mad^{me} Pasta in the opera of Medea [by Cherubini], *with portraits of Mad^{me} Pasta, Mad^{me} Caradori and Sig^{r}. Curioni.* [Lithographs.] John Hayter: London, 1827. 208*.a.10.

Hook, Theodore Edward (1788-1841)
Portrait sketch of Michael Kelly. Pen and ink. c.1825. 1879-6-14-763.

Kneller, Sir Godfrey (1646 or 1649-1723)
Henry Purcell, head. Black chalk drawing. c.1690. Formerly attributed to Kneller. 1885-5-9-1897.

Laroon, Marcellus, the younger (1679-1772?)
'Concert party in Montagu House' signed and dated 'Laroon fecit 1736'. Pencil drawing. 1959-7-11-2.

Lediard, Thomas (1714-93)
An exact and particular Description of the beautiful Illumination . . . to be represented in a Prologue and an Epilogue to the Opera

Julius Caesar in Egypt (by Handel) on the stage of Hambro' . . . June 9 . . . 1727. Printed by Philip Lewis Stromer: Hambro [Hamburg]. [1727.] With two scene engravings by C. Fritzsch after T. Lediard. 165.b.3. (Another copy in the Reference Division, British Library, 603.k.23(2).)

Meckenem, Israhel van (c.1445-1503)
Female harpist, with male lutenist. Engraving. W.II. 469. 119.
Female singer, with male lutenist. Engraving. W.II. 468. 115.
Female harpist, with male lutenist. Engraving. W.II. 473. 148.
Male organist (playing a portative), with woman working the bellows. Engraving. W.II. 468. 116.
Female bagpiper. Engraving. W.II. 474. 149.

Mercier, Philip (1689/91-1760)
'A music party'. c.1740. Drawing of a group including ladies playing harpsichord and guitar, a male cellist, and partly concealed, in the background, a flautist. A lady in the foreground has a music book open on her lap. 1905-4-14-43.

Metsu, Gabriel (1629-1667)
Man seated, playing a guitar. Chalk drawing. Gg.2-292.

Neyts, Gillis (1623-1687)
Lady seated, playing a lute. Pen and wash drawing. 1857-2-28-228.

Orlik, Emil (1870-1932)
Wilhelm Furtwängler. Engraving. c.1920. Two copies: (i) 1949-4-11-3974. (ii) inscribed in pencil from Furtwängler to the family of Paul Hirsch. 1980-7-6-38.
Gustav Mahler. Engraving. 1902. 1940-6-29-3.
Richard Strauss. Engraving. 1917. 1980-7-26-39.

Parmigianino (1503-1540)
Study of a woman playing the organ (? St. Cecilia). Pen and brown ink drawing. 1946-7-13-446.

Perugino, Pietro (c.1445-1523)
Angel playing a viol. Pen and ink drawing. After Perugino. Pp.1-29.
Angel playing a harp. Fine pen and light brown ink drawing. After Perugino. c.1520. 1895-9-15-464.

Pian, Antonio de (1784-1851)
Part of a numbered series of etchings by Norbert Bittner (1786-1851) after designs by A. de Pian, for intended operatic productions. 1886-9-27-9. Case 251 vol.3. (The etchings, which bear only titles, apparently form part of *Theater-Decorationen nach Originalskizzen des K. K. Hoftheatermalers Anton de Pian, gestochen und verlegt von Norbert Bittner.* Vienna, 1818.) The following is a list of the operas in this series, with the composers when attributable with certainty or fair conjecture:
Les bayadères (55,58,62), Catel
La clemenza di Tito (52,91), Mozart
Coriolan (99), Giuseppe Nicolini
La destruzione di Gerusalemme (87), Zingarelli
Don Giovanni (84), Mozart
Fernand Cortez (76), Spontini
Héléna (57), Méhul
Joseph (68), Méhul
Lodoiska (42,70), Cherubini
Medea (71), Cherubini
La molinara (43), Paisiello
Palmira (66), Salieri
Die Jugend Peter des Grossen (79), Weigl
Regulus (46,83), J. W. Michl
Richard Coeur de Lion (98,100), Grétry
Giuletta e Romeo (94), Zingarelli
Salem (90), Ignaz von Mosel
Sargines (65,75), Dalayrac
Soliman (96), Süssmayr
Tancredi (64), Rossini
La vestale (44), Spontini
Die Zauberflöte (49,59,73,82,92), Mozart

Pocock, Isaac (1782-1835)
Watercolour sketch for *Cavaliers and Roundheads*, play with songs and choruses, produced at Drury Lane October 1835. (Text, also by Pocock, apparently unpublished, but is found in Add. MS 42931 ff.712-35.) 1956-7-14-8.

Polidoro da Caravaggio (assistant of)
David before the Ark. Drawing, pen and brown wash, heightened

with white. c.1535. Procession, including players of a harp, a lira da braccio, shawm, cymbals, two cornua, tambourine. 1959-11-14-1.

Rowlandson, Thomas (1756-1827)
William Parsons and John Bannister as 'Solomon' and 'Steady' in Charles Dibdin's opera *The Quaker*, first produced 1775. Watercolour on black chalk. Burney Collection vol.1, p.55. no.125.

Sanquirico, Alessandro (1777-1849)
Sceniche decorazioni . . . pel dramma serie l'ultimo giorno di Pompei [by Giovanni Pacini]. [Eight coloured aquatints.] [Milan, 1827.] 242.t.13.

Scharf, George, the elder (1788-1860)
Drawings, vol.1. Pencil drawings.

f.46 'Mr. Hoffmeister an engraver from Baden' playing the zither; London, 1840; 'a Russian teacher of music' playing the guitar; 'jeune Monsieur Quantin', playing the flute, Cambrai 1812; 'Mr. W a clever German piano forte player'; M [François] Servais from Brussels (playing the violoncello) and [Karol] Lipinski (playing violin), 1836.

f.47 Drawings of various instruments, including serpent, bassoon, trombone, harp, pianoforte, violoncello.

f.48 Drawings of various pianofortes, with a sketch of 'Messrs Collard's show room at Cheapside'; a drawing of 'Melophoneon, a new pianoforte, corner of Mortimer and Portland Street, September 1842'.

Sketchbook. Pencil. 1900-7-25-120. Including Morris dancers, 1827 (14); German band, c.1830 (45); Italian musicians, 1837 (51).

Schäufelein, Hans Leonhard (c.1480-c.1540)
Two drummers and a fifer. Woodcut. c.1515. C.D.II. 34. 91. A feast, including one trumpeter, two fifers, and one drummer. Woodcut. c.1535. C.D.II. 53. 236.

Schmutzer, Ferdinand (1870-1928)
The Joachim Quartet [Joseph Joachim, Carl Haliř, Emanuel Wirth, Robert Hausmann], playing Beethoven's quartet op.59, no.3. Etching, 884 × 1127 mm, dated 1904. 1978-1-21-355.

Ter Borch, Gerard, the younger (1617-81)
Lady playing a lute at a table. Chalk drawing. 1846-5-9-204.

Tomkins, Charles (1757-?)
Old opera house (ie King's Theatre), Haymarket, from the east. Water colour with pen outline. c.1800. With seating plan. Case 20. vol.V. no.51.

The Triumph of Maximilian
The department possesses two bound copies of the woodcuts comprising this work. Each volume has a title-page reading:
Kaiser Maximilians I. Triumph. Le triomphe de Maximilian I. Imprimé à Vienne chez Matthias André Schmidt et se trouve à Londres chez J. Edwards. 1796.

In the first volume (shelf mark 158.a.5: 1845-8-9-789), the majority of the woodcuts, namely 1-83, 86-7, 95, 98, 102**, 108-9, 113, 124* and 125, have as watermark the imperial eagle with a sickle on its breast. This indicates that these woodcuts, although bound with the title-page and introductory text printed in 1796, are of the first edition printed in 1526.

The second volume (shelf mark Case 44: 1859-10-8-145-282) has a different, later watermark, and is entirely of the 1796 edition. There is another issue of the 1796 edition (on paper water-marked WOLFEG, and different from the preceding) in the Department of Printed Books, British Library, pressmark 1899.n.40.

Fourteen of the woodcuts, 3, 4, 18, 20, 22, 24, 26, 30, 77, 78, 79, 113, 114, 115, show musicians, and are by various artists, as follows: 3, 4, 18, 20, 22, 24, 26, 30, by Hans Burgkmair the elder (1473-1531); 77, 78, 79, sometimes attributed to Albrecht Altdorfer (c.1480-1538); 113, 114, 115, by Leonhard Beck (c.1480-1542).

The details of each woodcut are:

3 Three mounted fifers, headed by Anthony the fifer, of Dornstatt.

4 Five mounted drummers.

18 Three lutenists, headed by Artus and two rebec players, on a car.

20 Two crumhorn players, two shawm-players and one sackbut-player, Hans Neuschel the younger, on a car.

22 Paul Hofhaimer, the court organist, playing a positive

organ (with an assistant at the bellows), on a car, which also carries a regal.

24 Eight musicians, on a car, playing a bass-viol, harp, viol, one lute, one quintern, two Rauschpfeiffen, pipe with tabor.

26 Choir, with sackbut player and shawm player, on a car.

30 Fools, including a recorder-player, and a Jews' harp player, on a car.

77 Five mounted sackbut players, and five mounted shawm players.

78 Five mounted sackbut players.

79 Five mounted shawm players, and five mounted Rauschpfeiffen players.

113 Five mounted trumpeters and five mounted kettledrummers.

114 Ten mounted trumpeters.

115 Ten mounted trumpeters.

Turner, Joseph Mallord William (1775-1851)

Petworth House: watercolour sketches on blue paper. 1828?
The Library, with piano. T.B. CCXLIV - 16.
A woman playing the harp to a small company. T.B. CCXLIV - 28.
Musicians, including a flautist (?) and a violinist. T.B. CCXLIV - 34.
A woman playing a piano in the Library. T.B. CCXLIV - 37.
'A little music: evening' (Finberg's description). Includes (?) a harp on the right and a violinist standing in the centre. T.B. CCXLIV-43.

The Pantheon, Oxford Street, London, the morning after the fire, 15 January 1792. Watercolour over pencil. T.B. IX - A.

Uwins, Thomas (1782-1857)

William Crotch. Water colour and pencil. c.1820. 1858-6-26-18.
Charles Hague. Watercolour. c.1815. 1858-6-26-42.4.

Velde, Esaias van de (c.1590-1630)

Concert with singers, bass viol, lute, treble viol, harpsichord and flute. Red chalk drawing, with pen and sepia, and light washes of water colour. Attributed to van de Velde. Sloane 5226-59.

Victors, Jan (c.1620-after 1676)
Old man playing a hurdy-gurdy. Pen drawing. 1895-9-15-1342.

Watteau, Antoine (1684-1721)
Studies of half-length figures of a woman, and of a man playing a flageolet. Chalk drawing. 1891-7-13-13.
A seated man playing the violin. Chalk drawing. 1922-10-16-1.
Studies of a man playing the flute. Chalk drawing. 1868-8-8-1274.
Two studies of a man playing a guitar. Chalk drawing. 1868-8-8-1275.
Standing youth, holding up a tambourine. Chalk drawing. 1872-1-13-769.

Weiditz, Hans (before 1500-1536?)
Maximilian I hearing Mass at Augsburg, with choir grouped before a choirbook on a lectern, and organ. Woodcut. c.1520. C.D.II. 173.
Female lutenist with male harpist. Woodcut. C.D.II. 176. 97.

MISCELLANEA

A special group of prints and drawings is described in:

'The wind-band in England. 1540-1840', by Edward Croft-Murray, *Music and Civilisation*. Edited by Terence Mitchell, 1980, pp.135-80 (*British Museum Yearbook* 4).

The thirty reproductions, preceded by a catalogue raisonné, include works by Hans Holbein, Wenceslaus Hollar, Francis Barlow and George Scharf I. The text of the article relates the illustrations to contemporaneous printed or manuscript music in the British Library (Music Library, and Department of Manuscripts).

Illustrated music titles – There are two portfolios, both containing titles of the nineteenth century, and at the same shelf-mark: c.259. One has English titles, mostly Victorian, the other French titles. Some thirty-five artists are in each group, and the work of each artist is in a separate, named folder.

Portfolio XV of the 'Authorities for Artists' (Case 255) has a folder marked 'Instruments'. It includes prints and drawings of various specimens, European and oriental. One important group comprises drawings made for Burney's *General History*, vols.1 and 2. Some of them were not engraved. There is a MS index, possibly in Burney's hand, of twenty-seven items, headed 'Original drawings from antique sculpture, paintings and instruments. Rome 1770'. The miscellaneous etchings in this folder include two of monkey orchestras, unsigned.

DEPARTMENT OF COINS AND MEDALS

Only one published catalogue contains items of musical interest. This is:

Medallic Illustrations of the History of Great Britain and Ireland. Compiled by the late Edward Hawkins, and edited by Augustus W. Franks and Herbert A. Grueber. 1885, repr. Spink, 1969.

Vol.2 includes:

(i) A medal issued by the Academy of Ancient Music in 1750, inscribed: 'In acknowledgement of merit . . . Pepusch praeses'.

(ii) Six medals of Handel, issued for various English festivals and commemorations, from 1769 to 1859.

The collections contain other medals commemorating composers and musical events. Enquiries should be addressed to the Keeper.

DEPARTMENT OF GREEK AND ROMAN ANTIQUITIES

The collections of this department contain a variety of important objects relating to ancient music. They may be divided into two categories.

INSTRUMENTS AND REPRESENTATIONS OF INSTRUMENTS

(i) Reconstruction of lyre; found in Athens; dated to 5th century BC. 1816. 6-10. 501.

(ii) Two wooden *auloi*; found in Athens; dated to 5th century BC. 1816. 6-10. 502.

(iii) The two so-called Maenad *auloi*; provenance unknown; probably Roman, dating uncertain. 1884. 4-9. 5, and 1884. 4-9. 6.

(iv) Terracotta model of woman playing *kithara*; provenance unknown; c.200 BC. 1846. 9-25. 36.

(v) Terracotta model of woman playing *pandoura*; provenance unknown; c.300 BC. 1919. 6-20. 7.

(vi) Bronze horn or cornu; provenance unknown; probably Roman. 1839. 11-9. 50c.

(vii) Terracotta lamp in form of man playing *hydraulis* water organ; provenance unknown; 2nd or 3rd century AD. 1965. 10-11. 1.

(viii) Two small bronze cymbals; provenance unknown; dating uncertain. 1906. 4-12. 1.

(ix) Plate (*pinax*) showing warrior holding trumpet; 5th century BC. BM catalogue of vases B590. 1849. 6-20. 1.

(x) Vase showing Melousa and Musaios listening to Terpsichore playing harp; 5th century BC. BM catalogue of vases E271. 1849. 9-9. 7.

(xi) Bronze statuette of a man playing a side-blown horn; Campanian. c.470 BC. (Temple bequest.) Bronzes 223.

(xii) Terracotta model of a trumpet. From Mont Ventoux, France. Roman period. 1904.2-4.440.

All the above are displayed in the exhibition illustrating Greek and Roman life, except E271, which is in Ground Floor Room 5.

Literature

Higgins, R. A., 'Terracottas', *British Museum Quarterly*, XXXI, 1968-69, 119-120, pl.LVI (no.8 describes (vii) above).

Higgins, R. A., and Winnington-Ingram, R. P., 'Lute-players in Greek Art', *Journal of Hellenic Studies*, 1965, 62-71 (includes discussion of (v) above).

Howard, Albert A., 'The *aulos* or tibia', *Harvard Studies in classical Philology*, IV, 1893, 1-60 (includes discussion of (iii) above).

Landels, J. G., 'The Reconstruction of Greek Auloi', *World Archaeology*, vol.12, no.3, Feb. 1981, 298-303.

Roberts, Helen, 'Reconstructing the Greek tortoise-shell Lyre', *World Archaeology*, vol.12, no.3, Feb. 1981, 303-13.

Roberts, Helen, 'The technique of playing ancient Greek instruments of the lyre type', *British Museum Yearbook*, 4, 1980, 44-76.

Other representations of instruments are found in the following catalogues:

Catalogue of the Greek, Etruscan and Roman Paintings and Mosaics in the British Museum. By R. P. Hinks. 1933.

26 (p.15): a music lesson. Roman. Includes a woman holding a lyre.

92 (p.62): a young man with two flutes. Roman (of doubtful authenticity).

Catalogue of the Terracottas in the Department of Greek and Roman Antiquities. By H. B. Walters. 1903.

Besides no.(iv) on p.156, the index includes a dozen entries under 'flutes', and others under 'harp', 'lyre', 'dancing'.

Catalogue of Sculpture in the Department of Greek and Roman Antiquities of the British Museum. By F. N. Pryce. Vol.1. pt.1. Prehellenic and early Greek. Vol.1. pt.1. Cypriot and Etruscan. 1928,31.

The indexes to each part include entries under 'flute players', 'lyre players', 'tambourine players'.

VASES

Vases of the fifth century BC all made in Attica, illustrating the occurrence of music in Greek daily life. The following is a small selection:

(i) Red-figured vase, showing a music lesson; BM Catalogue of vases E171.

(ii) Black-figured vase, Panathenaic amphora showing music contest. BM Catalogue of vases B141.

(iii) Red-figured vase, showing symposium scene with woman playing *auloi.* BM Catalogue of vases E486.

(iv) Red-figured vase, showing *aulos* player accompanying athletes exercising. BM Catalogue of vases E164.

The collection is fully described in:

Catalogue of the Greek and Etruscan Vases in the British Museum. Vol.1, pt.1 by E. J. Forsdyke; Vol.1, pt.2 by H. B. Walters; Vol.2 by H. B. Walters; Vol.3 by Cecil H. Smith; Vol.4 by H. B. Walters. 1893-1925.

The indexes refer to numerous illustrations of musical scenes, under such headings as *auletes, citharist, crotala* (clappers), flutes, *magadis* (harp), trumpet, etc.

DEPARTMENT OF MEDIAEVAL AND LATER ANTIQUITIES

The collections contain a miscellaneous range of objects of musical interest – instruments; some important association pieces; busts; some representations of players; and records of performance in the form of admission tickets and tokens.

INSTRUMENTS

Bells – early Christian and medieval

Iron bell, partly coated with brass; with a clapper and moveable handle. Irish. 63, 1-20, 1.

Another, with a fixed handle. Found near Charlbury, Wychwood Forest, Oxon. 63, 1-20, 2,

Bronze bell, with loose egg-shaped clapper; the sides are flat, wide at the base and narrowing slightly upwards, arch-shaped at top. Front and back slightly concave. On top a ring-handle. 1945, 11-2, 1. Said to have been found at Fintona, Co. Tyrone, February 1832.

Bronze quadrangular bell, handle terminating in rude animal heads. 54, 7-14, 1. Found in Birr, Co. Offaly. Said to be the bell of St. Raudhan of Lorra, Co. Tipperary, who died in AD 534. Irish.

Iron bell in a bronze shrine, the upper part decorated with silver niello and enamels. 9th-10th century. 54, 7-14, 6. Said to be the bell of St. Cuillean, the brother of Cormac McCuillean, King, Bishop and scholar of Cashel, Co. Clare, who died in AD 908. Irish.

The collections contain other Irish bells, some of which are said to have associations with saints.

Bronze bell, engraved with a crucifix, Virgin and Child, St. George and the Dragon, and St. John the Baptist. Above, in a narrow band, the inscription 'Villyam STUK ESLAI'; with a loop handle. 88, 7-11, 1. From Pickering, Yorkshire. Probably 14th century, and possibly made for William de Stokesley of Whitby. (See *Proceedings of the Society of Antiquaries*, 1888, 69-71.)

Bronze bell with medallions on the sides and an inscription round it near the top: MARC LE SER HEFT MEI GHEGOTEN MVC LXXIV. Flemish. 1574. 95, 3-15, 1.

Bronze bell with grooved handle loop and iron clapper attached by a bronze wire passing through a hole near the base of the loop. 1926, 10-8, 1. Found at Abydos in a building known as the Osireion. Probably Coptic.

Bronze bell with loop at top; body ornamented by engraved lines. Clapper wanting. 1951, 7-6, 13. Bought at Smyrna, Turkey, in 1901. Perhaps Coptic.

Stringed instruments

Lyre, from the Sutton Hoo Ship Burial

Made of maplewood, numerous fragments, including an arm with six strings, remains of five poplar or willow pegs and two square gilt-bronze plaques with projecting birds' heads. Anglo-Saxon. 1939, 10-10.

Literature

Bessinger, Jess B., 'The Sutton Hoo Harp Replica and old English musical Verse', *Old English Poetry. Fifteen essays.* Edited by R. P. Creed. Brown University Press; Providence, 1967, pp.3-20.

Bruce-Mitford, Rupert (and others), *The Sutton Hoo Ship Burial*, 1975, vol.1, 436-57, 'The complete Inventory of the Finds'. By R. Bruce-Mitford and Marilyn E. Luscombe, Inv. 203.

Bruce-Mitford, Rupert, *The Sutton Hoo Ship Burial.* A handbook, 3rd ed. 1979. Fig.31, p.46 shows the reconstruction of the lyre, fig.30, p.43 the original fragments.

Bruce-Mitford, Rupert, and Bruce-Mitford, Myrtle, 'The Sutton Hoo Lyre, Beowulf, and the Origins of the Frameharp', *Antiquity*, XLIV, 1970. 7-13.

Lyre, from the Taplow Barrow

The fragments consist of two gilt-bronze escutcheons; part of a thin and tapering bronze plate of a shape congruent with that of the escutcheons and evidently serving as a back-plate over which the rivets from the zoomorphic plaques were clenched; six wooden fragments, four of which are part of the peg-arm and one of its end-joints. Anglo-Saxon. 83, 12-14.

The Sutton Hoo and Taplow Lyres, though only partially preserved, share distinctive features, and therefore help to define the essential characteristics of the Anglo-Saxon lyre. On the other hand, there are divergences which serve to broaden our knowledge of the instruments.

Wooden gittern
The body and neck made from a single piece of wood, and carved with decorative panels of foliage inhabited by huntsmen, foresters, beasts and grotesques. The instrument has violin-type finger-board and sounding board. The peg-box has a silver cover engraved with the arms of Queen Elizabeth I surrounded by the Garter and the badge of the Earl of Leicester surrounded by the Garter. English, early 14th century, with later alterations. 1963, 10-2, 1.

There is also a small wooden carving of an owl, so close in style to one of the winged beasts on the instrument that it must come from it. But as there is no place on the gittern where it fits, it must have belonged to one of the gittern parts cut back when the instrument was turned into a violin. 1963, 10-2, 1B.

Literature

Remnant, Mary, and Marks, Richard, 'A medieval Guitar', *British Museum Yearbook*, 4, 1980, 83-134.

Wind instruments

Ivory cornett, with silver mounts. ? early 17th century. 85, 5-8, 117.

Carved ivory oliphant. Byzantine. 11th-12th century. (Borrodaile bequest.) 1923, 12-5, 3.

Carved ivory oliphant. Byzantine. 10th-11th century. Decorated with scenes from the hippodrome at Byzantium. Later known as the 'Clephane Horn'. 1979, 7-1, 1.

Literature

Dalton, O. M., 'The Clephane Horn', *Archeologia*, LXV, 1914, 213-22.

Ivory oliphant. Byzantine. Probably 11th-12th century. Fitted in the 14th century with silver mounts, of which the upper one is decorated with hunting scenes, and with a leather baldric decorated with silver disks bearing the arms of the Scottish earldom of Moray. Later known as the 'Savernake horn'. 1975, 4-1, 1.

Literature

Camber, Richard, and Cherry, John, 'The Savernake Horn', *British Museum Yearbook*, 2, 1977, 201-11.

Mechanical instruments

Musical clocks

European carillon clock, with a ten-bell carillon, by Isaac Habrecht, Strasburg, dated 1589. 88, 12-1, 100.

Carillon clock, with quarter chimes played on thirteen bells, by Nicholas Vallin, London, dated 1598. CAI - 2139.

Musical clock, with a choice of two tunes on nine bells, by George Clarke, London, c.1750. CAI - 2061.

Table clock, including a 32-pipe mechanical organ, by George Lindsay, London, c.1760. CAI - 2135.

Table clock, with a choice of tunes, by George Clarke, London, c.1760. CAI - 2061.

Organ clock, with a selection of seven tunes on twenty-eight pipes, by Benjamin Vulliamy, London, c.1820. CAI - 2172.

Long-case clock, playing three verses of one of a choice of seven tunes, by Boyle, London, c.1850. 1964, 7-3, 1.

Japanese (all anonymous, 19th century).

Small mantel clock, containing a musical box action in the rectangular base. CAI - 2031.

Mantel clock, containing a musical box in the rectangular base. CAI - 2037.

Mantel clock, musical with six bells. CAI - 2038.

These three Japanese clocks are described by a former owner, J. Drummond Robertson, in his book, *The Evolution of Clockwork. With a special section on the clocks of Japan*, Cassell: London, 1931.

Musical watches

The collections contain a number of watches, which play musical tunes.

Musical boxes

(i) In a wooden case, with inlaid lid and detached winding-peg. Possibly Swiss, c.1850. O A 6548. The manuscript tune-sheet, which is headed: 'Mandoline, a Forte Piano', reads as follows (with added dates of composition, or publication, of the original).

1 Otello, Romance, Assisa a pie d'un salice. Rossini. [1816].
2 Portrait charmant, Romance par G. (= Germain) Delavigne [c.1835].
3 Beatrice di Tenda. Ma la sola ohime son io. Bellini. [1833].
4 Prague Walzer. Labitzky [ie his *Erinnerungen an Prag Walzer*, op.7, first published by Berra, c.1835].

The date of the box is suggested by the style of the winding mechanism, and the description at the head of the tune-sheet. (See John E. T. Clark, *Musical Boxes*, Cornish: Birmingham, 1948, pp.19,53,53, and Graham Webb, *The Cylinder Musical-Box Handbook*, Faber: London, 1968, pp.19,30,31 etc.)

(ii) In an inlaid walnut case, with a table stand of identical pattern. Made by Paillard Vaucher fils, Ste. Croix (Switzerland). no.13607. c.1870. 1980, 7-10. 1. The plate headed 'Mandoline Quatuor. Eight airs'.

REPRESENTATIONS OF PERFORMANCE

Two bone panels, forming part of a casket. Byzantine. 11th-12th century. 85, 8-4, 1-2.

The panels perhaps represent scenes from the hippodrome, the second showing dancers and musicians, one of whom blows an oliphant. (See O. M. Dalton, *Catalogue of Ivory Carvings of the Christian Era in . . . the British Museum*, 1909, no.16.)

Here may also be listed some ivory carvings which, though forming the covers of manuscripts in the collections of the British Library, Department of Manuscripts, are fully described only in Dalton's catalogue (see above).

Panel on the cover of a Carolingian psalter (Add. MS 37768).

Ivory. Rhenish. 12th century. King David playing an imaginary stringed instrument, perhaps intended to be a type of bowed lyre (rotte). (Dalton, no.613.)

Two panels on the cover of a psalter (Egerton MS 1139). Ivory. Byzantine. 12th century. The sixth medallion of the upper cover shows King David playing a dulcimer, with four musicians – two playing harps, one a vielle, and another a fiddle. (Dalton, nos.28,29.)

BUSTS AND ASSOCIATION PIECES

Charles Burney, the musical scholar (1726-1814):

A marble portrait bust by Joseph Nollekens, dated 1802. 1944, 7-4, 1.

George Bernard Shaw, the dramatist and musical critic (1856-1950):

A bronze portrait bust modelled by J. Caplans, 1955. 1955, 11-6, 1.

A bronze portrait bust modelled by Clare Winston, 1946. 1979, 10-1, 1.

Plaster death-mask, modelled by Charles Smith, 1950. 1977, 11-1, 1.

Vase commemorating Handel. English porcelain – Bow, c.1760: With three children typifying music, drama and dancing. The sides are divided into four panels, one of which includes a piece of music headed 'Minuette' arranged with a 'Song', a 'Waltz' and other music, in the form of an enamelled trophy. One panel is headed 'T F', probably the initials of Thomas Frye. 1938, 3-14-113.

The Bow factory issued other pieces commemorative of Handel, now in private collections. Two of them bear the date 1759 and both are decorated with a minuet identical to that mentioned above. One of these bears Handel's name.

The use of the word 'Waltz' seems to be early and antedates the earliest citation given in *OED* by some twenty years.

Literature

Bow Porcelain. 1744-1776. A special exhibition . . . to commemorate the bicentenary of the retirement of Thomas Frye, Manager of the Factory . . . October 1959-April 1960. (Catalogue by Hugh Tait.) 1959. Fig.36 illustrates the commemorative vase (no.104) which is described on p.41.

A silver watch, formerly the property of Handel. His name is inscribed on the outer case, which has repoussé ornament showing musicians. Made by Golling, Augsburg, prior to 1745. On show in 17th-18th century corridor, historical relics section. 1935, 10-24, 1.

THE MONTAGUE GUEST COLLECTION

This collection, which contains much of interest for the history of musical performance in the British Isles, is described in:

Catalogue of the Montague Guest Collection of badges, tokens and passes, presented in 1907. By A. B. Tonnochy, T. D. Kendrick, and C. F. C. Hawkes. pp.viii.206. pl. VIII. 1930.

Many of these items are made of gold, silver, bronze or ivory and are of considerable artistic merit. They relate, *inter alia*, to the King's Theatre, Haymarket; the Theatre Royal, Covent Garden; the Pantheon; Sadler's Wells; various music halls; London and provincial concerts and festivals, including Jullien's Promenade Concerts, the Crystal Palace, the Dublin Musical Society; and the London pleasure gardens of Marylebone, Ranelagh, and Vauxhall. One item of particular interest is a serial ticket for concerts including Corelli's music given in London, c.1740. The catalogue, which is arranged by institutions, events, etc., has no index, but a typescript index is available in the department.

DEPARTMENT OF PREHISTORIC AND ROMANO-BRITISH ANTIQUITIES

INSTRUMENTS

Horns

The British Museum's prehistoric collections include fifteen bronze age horns, some end-blown, some side-blown, from various sites in Ireland. These horns are listed as numbers 14A, 14B, 14T, 14U, 14V, 14W, 14X*, 14Y*, 14Z, 14Z1, 19A, 19B, 34, 45*, 46 (those marked with an asterisk being fragmentary) in the article by John M. Coles cited below under 'literature'. It gives a full description of each instrument, with the museum's registration numbers.

Trumpet

Bronze trumpet (mouthpiece), from Great Chesterford, Essex. 160 mm. Romano-British. 71, 12-31, 1.

Bone flutes

Two-hole flute, from Les Roches (Sergeac, Dordogne), from the Reverdit collection. 124 mm. Upper palaeolithic. Sturge collection.

Two-hole flute, from La Roque (Dordogne). 124 mm. ? later upper palaeolithic. (Condition suspicious.) Sturge collection.

One-hole flute, from Cambridge. 108 mm. Romano-British. 82, 3-21, 6.

Two-hole flute, no provenance. 116 mm. Romano-British. 66, 12-3, 204.

Two-hole flute, no provenance. 88 mm. Decorated. Romano-British.

Three-hole flute, from Cambridge. 75 mm. Romano-British. 82, 3-21, 7.

Rattles

Bell-shaped pottery rattle, decorated, from Rehfeld, East Germany. 116 mm. Lusatian culture. Bronze age. 68, 12-28, 217.

Globular gold rattle, from Ireland. 84 mm. Bronze age. 39, 3-27, 1.

Bronze flesh hook, from Dunaverny Bog, Co. Antrim. 620 mm. Late bronze age. 56, 12-21, 1. The shaft of the hook is pierced with seven rods, the top of each being attached to a bird, and the lower end of each fitted with a ring, from each of which a rattle was suspended.

Bronze rattle, in the shape of a flattened sphere, the rim pierced with eight holes for rattles attached by chains, five of which survive. From Hallstatt, Austria. 61 mm. Early iron age. 1916, 6-5, 273. (Illustrated in the article by Sir Hercules Read cited below.)

Literature

Coles, John M., 'Irish bronze age Horns and their Relations with Northern Europe', *Proceedings of the Prehistoric Society*, new series, XXIX, no.11, 1963, 326-56.

Holmes, Peter, 'The manufacturing Technology of the Irish Bronze Age Horns', in *The Origins of Metallurgy in Atlantic Europe*, edited by Michael Ryan, Dublin, [1979], with 15 plates. (Proceedings of the fifth Atlantic Colloquium.)

Megaw, J. V. S., 'Penny Whistles and Prehistory', *Antiquity*, XXXIV, 1960, 6-13.

Megaw, J. V. S., 'Problems and Non-problems in Palaeo-organology: a musical miscellany', *Studies in ancient Europe. Essays presented to Stuart Piggott*, edited by J. M. Coles and D. D. A. Simpson, Leicester, 1968, 333-58.

Read, Sir Hercules, 'On a collection of antiquities from the early iron age cemetery of Hallstatt, presented to the British Museum by Lord Avebury.' Introduction and inventory by Sir C. H. Read. Notes and chronology by Reginald A. Smith. *Archaeologia*, ser.2, XVII, 1916, 145-62. Pl.28, no.20, illustrates the bronze rattle listed above.

DEPARTMENT OF EGYPTIAN ANTIQUITIES

The collection of instruments is fully described in:

Catalogue of Egyptian Antiquities in the British Museum. III. Musical Instruments. By R. D. Anderson. Drawings by Grace Huxtable. pp.86. 1976.

The text includes 150 figures.

The instruments fall into eight groups – clappers; cymbals and crotals; bells; rattles; sistra; flutes and reed instruments; lutes; harps. The figures include some reproductions of carvings and tomb-paintings of musical scenes, and of a few figures playing musical instruments. Two notable scenes (EA 37981 and EA 37984) of the Eighteenth Dynasty, 1425 BC, show female musicians. A selection of the instruments is displayed in the Fourth Egyptian Room (Daily Life).

Literature

Duchesne-Guillemin, Marcelle, 'Music in ancient Mesopotamia and Egypt', *World Archaeology*, vol.12, no.3. Feb. 1981, 287-297.

DEPARTMENT OF ETHNOGRAPHY
(The Museum of Mankind, 6 Burlington Gardens, London W1X 2EX)

The collections of this Department are arranged according to four large areas – Africa, the Americas, Oceania and Asia; complemented by holdings of the recent folk-culture of Europe and the Near East. These collections contain a large number of musical instruments but there is no catalogue of them. (A summary outline is included in the introduction to *British Museum Yearbook* 4. See p.135.) Specific inquiries should be addressed to the Department, as above.

INSTRUMENTS

The Raffles Gamelan

A famous group of objects is the 'Raffles Gamelan', which was brought to England from Java in 1816 by Sir Stamford Raffles, and was presented to the British Museum by one of his sister's descendants in 1859. The gamelan is incomplete, comprising eighteen instruments or parts of instruments. These are possibly three hundred years old but their exact age cannot be determined at present.

Literature

The Raffles Gamelan. A historical note. Edited by William Fagg. With a biographical note by Douglas Barrett. pp.3, pl.16. 1970. Contents: 'Sir Stamford Raffles'. By Douglas Barrett. 'The Raffles Gamelan'. By William Fagg. 'Raffles on Javanese Music. I.' (Reprinted from a 'Discourse delivered at a meeting of the Society of Arts and Sciences, in Batavia', 24 April 1813.) 'Raffles on Javanese Music. II.' (Reprinted from his *History of Java*, London, 1817, vol.1, pp.469-72.) The frontispiece is a portrait of Raffles.

The gamelan is also described in a short, anonymous article in the *Illustrated London News*, 12 May 1860, 'Musical Instruments from Java'.

Rattles, etc. (transferred from the Department of Mediaeval and Later Antiquities, 1981)

Tsanatsel (brass sistrum). Ethiopic. 17th-18th century. 93, 11-11, 169.

Pair of brass rattles, fitted with numerous small bells of varying pitch. Ethiopic. 16th-17th century. 99, 4-21, 3.

Other literature

Anon, 'An ivory Drum from Benin', *British Museum Quarterly*, XXVII, 1963-4, 60.

Braunholtz, H. T., 'Carved Drum from New Guinea', *British Museum Quarterly*, IV, 1930, 14-15.

Braunholtz, H. T., 'A War Drum from Khartoum', *British Museum Quarterly*, XIII, 1938, 7-8.

Braunholtz, H. T., 'The Oldman Collection. Aztec gong, etc.' *British Museum Quarterly*, XVI, 1952, 54.

Fagg, William B., 'A Drum probably from the Ivory Coast', *British Museum Quarterly*, XV, 1952, 111-2.

Fagg, William B., 'Further Note on a West African Drum', *British Museum Quarterly*, XXI, 1957, 107.

Macleod, M. D., 'Music and Gold-Weights in Asante', *British Museum Yearbook*, 4, 1980, 225-42.

Montagu, Jeremy, 'The Conch in Prehistory: pottery, stone and natural', *World Archaeology*, vol.12, no.3, Feb. 1981, 273-9.

DEPARTMENT OF ORIENTAL ANTIQUITIES

INTRODUCTION

The cultural range of this department extends geographically from the lands of Islam to the sub-continent of India and the territories of South-East Asia, taking in Central Asia and Tibet on its northern boundary and reaching to China and Japan in the Far East. The musical objects in the collections date from prehistoric times right up to the early years of the present century. While most of the instruments are of types used in religious ceremonial, there are also a good many specimens intended for secular music-making. The representations of performance, in paintings, prints, and three-dimensional objects, are equally varied.

ISLAM

Oliphant. Ivory. 12th to 13th century AD. The mouth has a carved band showing oxen and deer, separated by ornamental patterns. With two silver mounts, each fitted with a suspension ring. O. A. + 1302.

Those Persian and Turkish manuscripts, in the form of albums, in the collections of the Department of Oriental Antiquities, which have miniatures of musical subjects, are included in the descriptive catalogues by Norah Titley listed above (p.121).

INDIA

Instruments (all from north-west India, c.2500 to c.1500 BC)

Clay whistle in the form of a bird. 1880-1348.
Clay ocarina. 1880-1347.
Clay flute. 1880-1346.

Literature

Knox, Robert, 'Three clay wind Instruments from ancient India', *British Museum Yearbook* 4, 1980, 77-82.

Representations – sculpture

Male musician with an arched harp. Terracotta relief. Central India. Gupta period. 5th century AD. 1969. 12-17. 1.

Railing pillar with double-pipe player. Central India. Mathura. 2nd century AD. 1965. 2-26. 1.

Stair-risers from Jamalgarhi. Carved in high relief with small figures. 2nd to 3rd century AD. Nos.30-34, 36, 37, 39, 40 include groups of musicians. 1880-30-61.

An image of Sarasvatī holding a *vina* (stick-zither). 12th to 13th century AD. 1872-7-1-55.

An image of Sarasvatī, surrounded by *kinnaras* with *vinas* (stick-zithers) and bells. Bengal. 12th century AD. 1872-7-1-32,33.

Representations – painting (arranged by schools)

Company school *(the first four all mid 19th century, on English paper watermarked 1827)*

Travelling musicians, with *ḍholak* (drum) and *thali* (clappers). 1884, 9-13, 31.

Conch-shell blower. 1884, 9-13, 59.

A *vina* (stick zither) player, and drummer. 1884, 9-13, 73.

Musicians with *shahnai* (shawm) and *pakhāvaj* (drum). 1884, 9-13, 78.

Conjuror carrying a *sarod* (lute). Late 18th century. 1974, 6-17, 07 (04).

A music master carrying a *sarod* (lute). Late 18th century. 1974, 6-17, 07 (14).

Two women musicians, each playing a *sindhi sarangi* (bowed lute). On ivory. 19th century. 1974, 6-17, 019 (5).

Deccan

Holi festival, with women musicians, two playing the *sarod* (lute), two the tambourine, two the *kasya* (small cymbals), one the *pakhāvaj* (drum). c.1750. 1920, 9-17, 057.

Woman musician, holding a *sarod* (lute). c.1800. 1955, 10-8, 093.

Nobleman playing the *vina* (stick-zither), watched by other musicians. c.1750. 1969, 3-17, 08.

Hairdarzedah of Bijapur, listening to musicians. 18th century. 1974, 6-17, 010 (49).

Mughal

Girl playing *vina* (stick-zither). 18th century. 1920, 9-17, 0188.

Wali Qalandar with a musician playing a *tamburā* (lute). 18th century. 1974, 6-17, 03 (44).

Court scene with dancers and musicians. Early 18th century. 1974, 6-17, 021 (66).

The 'Manley Ragamala', of c.1610, contains paintings in the Mughal style, some of which show musical performance, 1973, 9-17, 02-58.

Literature

Cran, Robert, '*The Manley Ragamala:* an album of Indian illustrated musical modes', *British Museum Yearbook* 4, 1980, 181-214.

Pahari

Scene from the Ramayana. Five musicians playing S-shaped trumpet, *karna* (straight trumpet), *naqqare* (drums), *ranasringa* (curved horn), *shahnai* (shawm). Basohli style. Late 18th century. 1923, 7-16, 07.

Birth of Rama. Including four musicians, playing *singa* (curved horn), *karna* (straight trumpet), *shahnai* (shawm), *naqqare* (drums). Guler style. c.1760. 1948, 10-9, 0123.

Rajasthan

From a Ragamala. Musicians playing *sarod* (lute) and *pakhāvaj* (drum). 1772. 1936, 4-11, 019.

Lady playing a *vina* (stick-zither). c.1770. 1966, 7-25, 010.

South India

Dancing girls with woman playing a *sarod* (lute) and a man playing a *pakhāvaj* (drum). c.1800. 1954, 10-9, 015.

BURMA

Bell. Brass. 19th century. 1880-276.
Bell. Bronze. Heavily inscribed. n.d. 1880-288.
Standing musician, with a *snè* (shawm). Wood. 18th century. 1842, 4-23, 24.
Standing musician, with a lute-type stringed instrument. Wood. 18th century. 1842, 4-23, 21.
Seated musician, with a *gandama* (double-headed drum) held vertically. Wood. 18th century. 1942, 4-23, 23.

CAMBODIA

Large Shan drum, with loop handles, surmounted by the figures of four frogs. Bronze. Laos? 17th century or later. 1903-3-27-6.
Pair of small Shan drums, each surmounted by the figures of four frogs. Bronze. Laos? 17th century or later. 1954-7-15-29,30.

JAVA

Bells (all from the Raffles collection)

Bell with ovoid openwork body. Bronze. District of Kedu. 1859-12-28-106.
Bell with ovoid openwork body. Bronze. District of Kedu. 1859-12-28-107.
Bell with ovoid openwork body. Bronze. District of Kedu. 1859-12-28-108.
Bell with ovoid openwork body, terminating at one end in elephant's head. Bronze. 1859-12-28-109.
Bell with ovoid openwork body, and projecting dragon's head. Bronze. 1859-12-28-110.
Ritual bell. Bronze. 13th century. 1859-12-28-111.
Ritual bell with clapper. Bronze. 13th century. 1859-12-28-112.
Bell, lacking clapper. Iron. 1859-12-28-113.

Bell, lacking clapper. Iron. 1859-12-28-114.
Ritual bell with Vajra finial. Bronze. District of Kedu. 13th century? 1859-12-28-115.
Ritual bell with Vajra finial. Bronze. 10th-11th century. 1859-12-28-116.
'Knobbed' bell with Y-slit below, surmounted by a ring. Bronze. 1859-12-28-117.

THAILAND

Bell. Bronze. 17th century or later. 1954, 7-15, 26.
Elephant bell. Bronze. 17th century or later. 1954, 7-15, 27.
Bell. Gilt bronze. 17th century or later. 1954, 7-15, 28.

CENTRAL ASIA

The Stein collection includes representations of musical performance of various kinds. A description of them is found in: Aurel Stein, *Serindia*, Oxford University Press; Oxford, 1921. Vol.III includes, on pp.1467-9, 'Appendix H. Notes on the musical instruments represented in the Stein Collection. By Kathleen Schlesinger. I. Musical instruments represented in paintings from the 'Caves of the thousand Buddhas', Tun-Huang. II. Musical instruments represented in terracotta figurines. III. Remains of musical instruments.' The paintings, which are on silk and date mostly from the late 8th or early 9th century AD, form the subject of two more recent books mentioned below. The terracottas date mostly from the 2nd to 3rd century AD and comprise both human and monkey musicians. These representations and the fragments of instruments, are described by Schlesinger in some detail, but are mostly denoted only by the roughly equivalent European terms. Some of the terracottas are reproduced on pl.I-III of the volume of plates in *Serindia*, with reference numbers which relate to the text. There is also a summary description of the musical terracottas in vol.1, p.99, again with some references to the plates.

The Dunhuang Buddhist paintings (the 'paradise paintings') are the subject of:

A Catalogue of Paintings recovered from Tun-Huang by Sir Aurel Stein . . . preserved in the Sub-Department of Oriental Prints and Drawings in the British Museum and the Museum of Central Asia Antiquities, Delhi. By Arthur Waley. 1932.

Those paintings preserved in the British Museum comprise nos.I-CCLXXI of this catalogue, whose index does not list musical subjects. The following are the numbers, with page references, of those which show musical performance:

I, p.1 Four musicians, playing *ch'in* (zither), *po-pan* (clappers), *sheng* (mouth organ), and *pi-pa* (lute).

XII, p.20 Dancer, and musicians, playing *hsiao* (end-blown flute), *pi-pa* (lute), *k'ung hou* (harp), *po-pan* (clappers), *ti-tzu* (side-blown flute), *sheng* (mouth organ), *k'ung hou* (harp), *ti-tzu* (side-blown flute).

XXXI*, p.52 Three souls, playing *ti-tzu* (side-blown flute), *sheng* (mouth organ), and *po-pan* (clappers).

XXXIII, p.54 Two musicians, playing *ti-tzu* (side-blown flute) and *sheng* (mouth organ).

XXXV*, p.60 Musicians and dancers.

XXXVII, p.62-3 Eight musicians, playing *yao-ku* (waisted drums), *ti-tzu* (side-blown flute), hour-glass drum, *t'ao-ku* (drum) and two-sided rattles, *pi-pa* (lute), *k'ung-hou* (harp), *hsiao* (end-blown flute), *sheng* (mouth-organ).

LXX, p.107 Six musicians.

LXXXVI, p.119 Three musicians, playing *yao-ku* (waisted drum), *hsiao* (end-blown flute), and tambourine.

XCII, p.122 Three musicians, playing *ti-tzu* (side-blown flute), *hsiao* (end-blown flute) and *po-pan* (clappers).

XCVIII, p.126 Dancer with three musicians, playing *po-pan* (clappers), *hsiao* (end-blown flute), and *pi-pa* (lute).

The above musical scenes are reproduced in colour in *The Art of Central Asia, (The Stein Collection).* vol.1 *Paintings from Dunhuang*, by Roderick Whitfield. Kodansha: Tokyo, 1982.

TIBET

Bells

Dril-bu (decorated ritual bell). ? bronze. 18th-19th century. 1948, 7-16, 11.

Lutes

Sgra-snyan (long-necked lute)

There are a number of specimens in the collections, some ornamented, all probably of the 19th century:

- (i) With a peg-box carved in the shape of a horse's head. Christy 94-385.
- (ii) Another, similar. Christy 94-381.
- (iii) With peg-box carved in the shape of a human head. Christy 94-380.
- (iv) With incised decoration on the body. Christy 94-384.
- (v) With decorative painting on the body. Christy 94-382.

Pipes

Gling-bu (double pipe). ? apricot wood. From Ladakh. 19th century. Christy 4813.

Trumpets

Dung-dkhar (conch trumpet)

The collections include a pair, each with gilt mouthpiece and metal extension of the valve, and each decorated with coloured stones and glass. 18th century. 1933. 5-10.1 (a, b).

Single conches are:

- (i) With metal mouthpiece and tubular extension, partly gilt, and with attached panel with a gilt *makara* (sea monster) in its centre. 1954. 2-227.
- (ii) With inscriptions in Tibetan, Chinese and Manchu on attached panel. 18th century. 1880-1074.
- (iii) With brass panel. 19th century. 1948-7-16-7.
- (iv) With brass panel. 19th century. 1905-5-19-99.

Rkang-gling (short trumpet)

(i) Copper with two embossed brass mouthpieces and central band, the bell in the form of a dragon's head. 19th century. 1910. 6-16. 4.

(ii) Copper with contrasting brass. 19th century. 1905. 5-19. 131.

Pair of trumpets, consisting of a length of bone bound with silver wire, with mouthpiece, central band and curved bell, all of silver. The metal sections set with turquoises. 19th to 20th century. 1933. 5-8. 36 (a,b).

Rkang-gling (*yogins*, thigh-bone trumpet)

(i) Pair, decorated with bronze mounts. 19th century. 1921-2-19-15,16.

(ii) Single trumpet, mounted in silver, with suspension rings. 19th to 20th century. 1933. 5-8, 35.

Dung-chen (telescope trumpet)

(i) A pair, each some 12 metres long, in 3 sections. Copper, with rings of applied silver and bands of silver decoration at the bell end. 19th to 20th century. MM 1978. As.13 (1-2).

(ii) Single trumpet, some twelve metres long, in 3 sections. Copper with brasswork decoration. 19th to 20th century. 1933. 5-8. 38 (a).

A pair of large curved trumpets. 19th century. 1880-371.

Shawms

Rgya-gling, a pair. Wood covered with silver, with gilt bands set with coral and turquoise. With 7 finger holes and 1 thumb hole, and metal bell. Tibet or Nepal. 19th century. 1946-7-13-12.13.

Sor-na. A plain wooden shawm. 19th century. 1880-371.

Drums

Damaru (hour-glass drum), with textile band and clappers, and case made of wool. 19th century. 1933. 5-8. 86.

Thöd rnga (skull drum) made of two skull tops, with leather band and strap round the middle. 19th to 20th century. 1919. 473.

Rnga and *yob* (drum and crooked stick). 18th to 19th century. 98-6–22-33.

Cymbals

Gsil-snyan (small cymbals)
- (i) 19th century. 1913-11-3-97,97a.
- (ii) 19th century. 94-3-10.87.
- (iii) With a tassel. 19th century. 1910-6-28-16.

Rol-mo (loud cymbals)
- (i) Two pairs. 19th century. 1905-5-91-103, and 1905-1-18-2.
- (ii) With case. 19th century. 1894. 3-10.7.

Jew's harp

Two sets, one in a tubular container of carved wood. Christy 95-246,247.

Literature

Zwalf, W., *Heritage of Tibet*, 1981, 88-93.

Zwalf, W., and Oddy, W. A., *Aspects of Tibetan Metallurgy*. Research Laboratory and Department of Oriental Antiquities, 1981. (British Museum Occasional Paper no.15).

CHINA

Instruments

Rattle

Bronze, gourd-shaped musical instrument, perhaps a rattle, with curved handle surmounted by an ox. 3rd-2nd century BC. From Liangwangshan, Yunnan province. 1950. 4-5, 1 (14).

Bells (bronze)
- (i) *Nao*. Shang dynasty. 13th-11th century BC. 1953. 10-24. 1 (3).
- (ii) *Zhong*. Early Eastern Zhou period. 8th-7th century BC. 1961. 2-14. 2 (9).
- (iii) *Zhong*. Late Western Zhou period. 8th century BC. 1973. 7-26. 22 (9).
- (iv) *Zhong*. Eastern Zhou period. 6th-5th century BC. 1936. 11-18. 5 (12).

Z, (v) *Zhong.* Eastern Zhou period. 6th-5th century BC. 1973. 7-26. 23 (12).

Z, (vi) *Zhong.* Eastern Zhou period. 6th-5th century BC. 1958. 5-15. 1 (12).

Z, (vii) *Zhong.* Late Eastern Zhou period. 6th-5th century BC. 1957. 2-18. 1.

Z, (viii) *Zhong.* Eastern Zhou period. 5th century BC. Said to have been found at Ji xian, Honan province. 1965. 6-12. 1 (15).

Zl (ix) *Zhong.* Eastern Zhou period. 4th-3rd century BC. 1935. 1-15. 17 (14). Late Eastern Zhou period, possibly from Changsha. With a design of dragons against a granulated background. 1979. 10-10. 7.

Cl (x) Chariot bell. Eastern Zhou period or Han dynasty. 1973. 6-20. 6.

(xi) Decorated with a frog. 1st century BC. From Liang-
Wi wanshan, Honan province. 1948. 10-13. 15 (14).

Be (xii) With archaistic design. Ch'ing dynasty. O.A. + 6623.

(xiii) Bell-shaped ornament. Bronze, inlaid with gold and silver. Archaistic, possibly Ming dynasty (1368-
La 1644 AD). 1973. 7-26. 82.

La (xiv) Large bell. K'ang-hsi 60 (1722 AD). 1867. 7-22. 1.

(xv) Large bell given by Queen Victoria. Taokuang 19 (1839 AD). 1844. 3-9. 1.

Representations

Ti-tsu (side-blown flute). Blanc de chine, in imitation of bamboo. Two specimens, both 18th century AD. 1980-7-28-637 and 1980-7-3-638.

Three female musicians, playing clappers (not represented), *pi-pa* (lute) and *hsiao* (end-blown flute). Glazed earthenware. Tang dynasty, 7th century AD. 1936. 10-12. 53-55 (25).

JAPAN

Instruments

Stringed instruments

Samisen (lute). 19th century. 1933. 3-1593.

Samisen (lute) with tassel. 19th-20th century. 1928. 7-10 3.

Wind instruments

Yokobue (side-blown flute)

(i) In plain lacquered paper container. 18th century. 1969. 5-27 1.

(ii) In decorated lacquered case, with tassel. Late 19th century. 1945. 10-17 491.

(iii) In decorated lacquered case, with tassel. Late 19th century. 1945. 10-17 492.

Sho (mouth organ)

(i) Mid 18th century, with 3 books of music copied by a court official in 1804. 1934. 12-5 39.

(ii) Mid 19th century. 1928. 7-10 1.

(iii) A bamboo toy instrument. 19th century. 1969. 5-27 2.

Sankha (Buddhist ritual conch shell trumpet). Decorated in the 19th century. Signed: Myoguokusai. O A 7252.

Drums

Mokugyo (slit-drum)

(i) Large drum. 19th century. 91. 11-20 14.

(ii) Small drum. ? 19th century. O. A. + 1271.

(iii) Small drum, with bamboo striker. 19th century. O. A. + 7285.

Kotsuzumi (hourglass drum)

(i) Black lacquered body. Second half of 19th century. 1969. 5-27 3.

(ii) Green lacquered body. Second half of 19th century. 1968. 5-27 4.

(iii) Miniature representation, on a pouch ornament. Copper gilt. 19th century. 93. 2-5 133.

Buddhist ritual gong Decorated bronze, gilt. 16th century. 95. 10-19 1.

Miscellaneous

Bronze mirror, with bells on the circumference. 6th century. O. A. + 544.

Priest's staff, with finial fitted with jingles. 1928. 10-6 23.

Furitzutsu (shaking wand), fitted with bells and tassel: used in exorcism at Shinto festivals. 18th century. 1969. 5-27 12.

Sword furniture

Fragments of tin-bronze bells for the handle of a ritual sword. 5th to 6th century. O. A. + 1244.

Miniature metal ornaments, all probably 19th century.

(i) Woman playing a *koto* (board zither). 1951. 11-14 5.

(ii) *Biwa* (lute). 1951. 11-14 3.

(iii) Nobleman on a horse playing a *fue* (side-blown flute). 1951. 11-14 66.

Representations – *Netsuke*

Some specimens of musical interest in the collections are recorded in: Barker, Richard, and Smith, Lawrence, *Netsuke. The miniature sculpture of Japan.* (Illustrated) pp.184. 1976.

21. Seated monkey, holding a bamboo stick with an ivory plectrum, in imitation of a *samisen* player. Wood. Signed: Tomochika. 19th century. F.679. Franks collection.

171. Fox with *kotsuzumi* (hour-glass drum). Wood. Signed: Ittan. 19th century. F.245. Franks collection.

219. Boy playing a *fue* (side-blown flute). Ivory. Signed: Otoman. 19th century. F.663. Franks collection.

254. Yoshimasa, playing a *fue* (side-blown flute). Ivory. Signed: Unsei. 19th century. F.949. Franks collection.

339. The Chinese Emperor Ming Heian and his concubine Yang Kinei-Fei sharing a *fue* (side-blown flute). Ivory. Unsigned. 18th century. 1945. 10-17, 95.

354. Chinaman holding a trumpet-like instrument. Ivory. Unsigned. 18th century. F.558. Franks collection.

Representations – prints

The collection of Japanese prints includes a good many which contain scenes of musical performance. Reference should be made to: Harris, T. V., 'Musical Scenes in Japanese woodblock Prints', *British Museum Yearbook* 4, 1980, 215-24. This is a list, with an introduction and some specimen illustrations, of 82 prints by 38 artists, and with registration numbers. The prints date from the Edo period, 1603 to 1867.

Besides the prints listed by Harris, some others of musical interest are:

Keisai Eisen (1790-1848)
6 geisha singing and playing on a balcony. Triptych. 1906, 12-20, 310.
Doll musicians. 1902, 2-12, 292-296.

Isoda Koryūsai (fl.1760-1780)
Young man playing a *yokobue* (side-blown flute). *Hashiratake.* 1907, 5-31, 370.

Utagawa Kunichika (fl.1850)
Girl holding a *shakuhachi* (curved flute). 1902, 2-12, 347.

Utagawa Kunisada (1786-1864)
Genji playing a *yokobue*. 1906, 12-20, 1073.
Genji with *yokobue*. 1906, 12-20, 1079.
Priest blowing a *sankha* (conch-shell trumpet). 1906, 12-20, 1092.

Kitao Masanobu (1761-1816)
Woman playing a *samisen* and singing. 1909, 4-6, 467.

Utagawa Sadahide (fl.1850)
Girls playing *samisen* and *koto*. 1902, 2-12, 353.

Toyokuni (1769-1825)
Woman holding a *biwa* (lute). 1860, 4-14, 314.

Utamaro (1753-1806)
Boy dancing to a *samisen* player. 1906, 12-20, 336.

Among prints by various artists in an album of small *surimono* is one by Hokusai, showing girls playing *koto, samisen* and *yokobue.* Jap. album 42.

Representations – paintings
(The numbers are those of the Japanese paintings collection.)

Sumiyoshi Hirosada (19th century)
Lady playing a *biwa* (lute). 268.
Courtiers and ladies enjoying boating and music. 270,271.

Magawa I-itsu (19th century)
The Imperial orchestra, showing five musicians playing *taiko* (barrel drum), *kakko* (barrel drum), *sho* (mouth-organ), *oteki* (side-blown flute), and *fue* (flute). 286.

Itaya Keishu (18th century)
Benten playing a *biwa* (lute). 161.

Keizan (19th century)
Princess playing a *koto* (board zither). 2084.

Tosa Mitsunari (17th century)
Room, with *biwa* (lute) on the floor. 113.

Hishikawa Moronobu (late 17th century)
Ladies playing various instruments. 1376.
Musicians and dancers on a pleasure boat. 1374.

Renzan
Girls playing on various instruments. Dated 1838. 2009.

Tosen (early 19th century)
Seven sages occupied with reading, music, etc. 2035.

KOREA

Bell. Bronze. With dragon head and four asparas. Koryo period. c.13th century. 1966. 2. 21. 1.
T'aep yongso. (Shawm). Wood and brass. 19th century. 7411. (K.).

DEPARTMENT OF WESTERN ASIATIC ANTIQUITIES

The musical objects in the collections of this Department range from the third millenium BC to the early centuries of the Christian era. They are listed and described in:

Ancient musical Instruments of Western Asia in the Department of Western Asiatic Antiquities in the British Museum. By Joan Rimmer. pp.51. pl.xxv, 12 fig. 1969.

Appendix 1 comprises a classified list of 'Musical instruments and monuments representing musical instruments'. The instruments shown in the plates are lyres, rattles, bells, cymbals and clappers. A variety of musical scenes is shown in the reproductions of terracottas, bronzes and an ivory pyxis. They include lute-players, harpists, musicians with zithers, tambour and several kinds of pipes. The plates of reliefs illustrate players of lyres, vertical and horizontal harps, pipes and drums.

A reconstruction of the 'Silver lyre' (c.2600 BC) is on exhibition in the Babylonian Room.

Literature

Barnett, Richard D., 'New Facts about musical Instruments from Ur', *Iraq*, 31, 1969, 96-103.

Collon, Dominique, and Kilmer, Anne Draffkorn, 'The Lute in ancient Mesopotamia', *British Museum Yearbook* 4, 1980, 13-28.

Duchesne-Guillemin, Marcelle, 'Music in ancient Mesopotamia and Egypt', *World Archaeology*, vol.12, no.3, 1981, 287-97.

Mitchell, Terence, 'An Assyrian stringed Instrument', *British Museum Yearbook* 4, 1980, 33-42.

Poroda, Edith, 'A cylinder Seal showing a Harpist', *British Museum Yearbook* 4, 1980, 29-32.

INDEX

An asterisk denotes a portrait. The names of photographers are grouped together under 'photographers'.